MW01292361

# THE

# ALLIGATOR'S

# TOOTH

## STORIES FROM JAMAICA

## SHERRY KEITH

For the few who I
funny friend, who I
hope I will put her
stories into a book that
I can read.

Sherry
December 2013

ISBN:1480290750
ISBN-13:9781480290754

For Ariel and Zahava

# CONTENTS

# ACKNOWLEDGMENTS

Well deserving of thanks are Britt Ellerston, Carissa Peterson and Alice Reigert for their careful reading and proof reading of the text. Friends, Suzanne Girot and Pat Flynn, took much appreciated quick, but penetrating looks at the original title and contents giving me some important feedback. Special gratitude goes to Courtney Smith who, with her excellent technical formatting and final editing skills, moved this project from "almost finished" to a completed book. Also thanks to Robert Girling for suggestions and added details provided while listening to the stories being read aloud over breakfast or lunch on our deck. For digital photography, credit goes to Chris Rosales and Gary Palmer of San Francisco State University's audio-visual department who were willing to lend their well-honed technical skills. Added gratitude goes to Anabel Foster-Davis for several family photographs from the Jamaica years. The tropical scene on the cover is an original painting by Robert Girling.

# PREFACE

The desire to tell stories hit me sometime in my early fifties. Having worked many years as a social scientist, I was searching for another voice to sing of the adventures that took place during the eight years of my life stretching from 1968 to 1976. At the same time, I realized that all the dreams and ambitions of my youth had been more than fulfilled. In 1968, there was no way to anticipate how my life would be catapulted forward by the tides of history including de-colonization, the early stages of globalization, the women's movement, the Vietnam and Cold wars together etched with an overarching attitude of revolt against authority and tradition that were embodied in the 1960s and 1970s.

Towards the end of the 20th century, I'd come up against the limits of life plans drawn up so many years ago. These plans didn't include any guidelines for the decades which lay ahead. Searching everywhere for role models – female role models in particular – to inform the coming years of my life, I began devouring the flood of biographies and memoirs being published by and about women. While fascinating, most of these focused on women whose experiences had been quite different than my own.

Very few women of my generation who married young—I was twenty-one—were still married to the same person forty years later. Even fewer had spent the decade of their twenties living in the "Third World", pursued graduate studies and started a career while raising a family. Patterns like these became more commonplace in the last decades of the twentieth century.

Over the years, young women—mostly my students—frequently inquired how I managed to combine career, family, marriage with such an exciting life? I had never really thought much about having invented a recipe until my daughter had children of her own. Thrust into a new role, that of "the grandmother", history, including my own, caught up with me. Thinking about my grandchildren, knowing that my own children were too young to remember the details of those wonderful and arduous years of cooking up a life together with my husband when neither of us recognized any limits on what we could or might choose to do, I decided to begin writing stories about the Jamaica years intermingled with graduate studies in the United States.

While *The Alligator's Tooth* doesn't offer a life formula, I hope that it does give the reader a sense of  some key ingredients: dreams, ambitions, challenges, excitement, and compromise along with openness to adventure and opportunity that went into the mix of making a life which became mine.

Sherry Keith
Berkeley 2012

# THE ALLIGATOR'S TOOTH (1968 - 1970)

*Dear Ariel and Zahava,*

*I have been trying to decide where to begin these stories. Since I didn't want to go back to the beginning of time, I will start with the moment when Grandpa Robert and I made up our minds to go to Jamaica. That which came before and after this, I will tell you about later.*

*Granny Sherry*

# A TRAVEL POSTER

Searching for a flat in London is no fun. Especially, when you're looking ahead at an English winter. Most of the flats we examine are worn out bedsitters with threadbare couches, scuffed chairs and scratched tables. Small gas heaters requiring frequent feedings of shilling coins will be the only protection against the cold. After the summer in Spain, London seems large and lonely. Anna Kay and several Jamaican friends have moved back to the West Indies, so we are without contemporaries in this big, often bleak city.

The search persists day after day. The air chills, a reminder of the winter marching toward us. This does little to lift our spirits. I recall having just left a dingy little bedsitter with a shared loo down the hall in an outlying London neighborhood. The sun shone weakly through the foggy October afternoon. We decided to take the underground to downtown

London to find a cheap Indian restaurant for lunch. The spicy kick of Indian food suits Robert, while I still have not completely learned to appreciate pepper. As we emerge from the Charring Cross Underground station to scout for a restaurant, a travel poster catches my eye. The gentle curves of a white sand beach banded by a wide ribbon of turquoise dissolving into deep blue defy the London gray. Coconut palms with shaggy yellow-green fronds cast soft shadows on shimmering sand while two empty orange chaise lounges relax in tropical luxury. Below the picture, in heavy bold block letters, I read the word **"JAMAICA."**

"Is that where you come from?!," I shoot an undeniably rhetorical question Robert's way.

"Yah, I guess so," he replies vacantly without stopping to look at the poster.

This is the moment when Jamaica begins to take a definite shape in my mind.

"So, do you think we could go there?" On the edge of winter, jobless and almost without resources, taking our chances in some tropical paradise might be a better option than London. Robert raises his bushy Albert Einstein eyebrows with interest and looks back at the poster. We make a perfectly synchronized about-face and enter the travel agency to make inquiries.

"We'd like to find out about passages to Jamaica," Robert nods towards the travel poster in the large plate glass window.

A gray haired woman wearing a lavender sweater accented with black-fringed silk scarf, smiles curiously at us,

"When would you like to depart and return?"

We look at each other questioningly. This idea is clearly not yet a plan. We attempt a quick conversation via face making, shoulder shrugging and mental telepathy.

"Well, maybe next week," Robert offers tentatively.

"And the time of return?" the travel agent seems to be doing her best to take us seriously.

"One way," the definitive tone of his statement surprises all three of us!

The agent begins to scrutinize the thick blue covered binder oozing with printed airline schedules for hundreds of destinations.

"Let me see here. Well there's a BOAC (British Overseas Airways Corporation) flight Tuesdays, Thursdays and Saturdays. The Tuesday flight leaves Gatwick at 11:20 in the morning and arrives in Montego Bay at 6:40 p.m.,"

"We need to go to Kingston," Robert indicates politely. Harry Belafonte's honey voice floats in my ears,

> *Down the way where the nights are gay*
> *And the sun shines daily on the mountain top*
> *I took a trip on a sailing ship*
> *And when I reached Jamaica I made a stop*

"The Tuesday and Saturday flights continue from Montego Bay to Kingston and arrive at 8:45 p.m."

We nod with approval.

"How much does it cost?"

In the crispest of British accents, the travel agent delivers the dismal news,

"The one-way fare is just under 200 pounds, one hundred ninety seven pounds, five to be exact."

Well, there goes that great idea, I think, knowing that our net worth at that exact moment is less than one hundred ninety seven pounds, five, and we need twice that amount to buy the tickets.

Robert, however, appears to be undaunted.

"Is there space for next Tuesday?"

The agent calls to check on availability. After some minutes, she relays an affirmative reply.

"Shall I book the tickets?" The look on her powdered face reveals a trace of skepticism. Fortunately there aren't any other customers waiting to make inquiries about trips to Jamaica or elsewhere, so we aren't entirely wasting her time.

"No, not right now, we need to make some more inquires," Robert responds.

I keep quiet. Jamaica is Robert's territory. My knowledge, casually gleaned from a few family stories I've heard and conversations with Anna Kay and her friends in London is scant. We walk out of the travel agency into the cool London afternoon.

"Let's call my Aunt Mignon's brother, Manny, and go talk with him about going to Jamaica," Robert suggests.

Manny's secretary reports that he is out of the office until 3 o'clock. We find an Indian restaurant, stop there and dive into a hot plate of chicken curry. When we arrive at Manny's office, he has just returned from a round of golf. The London representative of the Jamaica Industrial Development Corporation, his easy salesman pitch for Jamaica charms us within seconds.

"Yes, mon, you should go to Jamaica. You will find a job, no problem at'tal."

We leave his office decided. He generously offers us the use of a flat belonging to a distant relative who isn't in London at the moment. We accept and stay the night to get our travel plans organized the following day.

In the morning, we go back to the BOAC office to make reservations for our air passage. Robert figures that we can charge the cost of the one-way tickets to the Barclay cards given to us by the bank when we arrived in England a little over one year ago.

The travel agent checks with Barclays when we give her the card to make the purchase.

"You need to go by the bank and speak with the manager," she tells us.

So we walk briskly to the branch and speak with the designated manager, a thin man wearing John Lennon spectacles.

"Jamaica, eh? You are going there to work and have family there?"

"Yes," we insist, which is, of course, the truth.

"All right then. I'll approve the charge if you surrender the cards."

"That's fine," we agree readily.

The travel date is set for the following Tuesday, October 18. We leave the bank in a cloud of excitement, rushing to purchase the tickets. Then we return to the flat to collect our things. We will head back to Colchester for the remaining days.

We call Robert's grandparents, Ruby and Stanton, in Kingston. They seem as excited as we are about our arrival.

"I'll tell David to pick you up at the airport, m'love" Granny Ruby promises.

# WAKING UP IN
# JAMAICA

October 18, 1968 Robert and I arrived in Jamaica. We flew all day and on into night away from the rainy, cold autumn of England. Jamaica first appeared as a scattering of lights in the darkness below as the plane nosed downwards, then bounced onto the runway. Immediately passengers began to rustle impatiently, jostling bags and overstuffed hand luggage, jockeying for position in the line of bodies that had begun to bleed out of the plane. Stepping out of the airplane into the Jamaican night, unrecognizable tastes and smells filled my mouth, lungs and nostrils. The dark sky immediately covered me like a warm, wet blanket. The soupy air dripped with smells I couldn't, as yet, name. The air felt so thick that I waved my hand against it to see if I could actually push it away. That first breath of Jamaica remains one of my most palpable memories.

The crowd of tired passengers surged forward towards a low-slung building. An incomprehensible mélange of chatter, laughter, exclamations and expletives rose like a steam cloud above a crowd of people on an open observation deck overlooking the airfield. A flock of sheep, we simply followed the human flow ahead towards the immigration check booths.

By the time we entered the dizzying customs area crushed with hundreds of people, each one gathering up what seemed to be extraordinary numbers of suitcases, packages and boxes, David had spotted us. We must have been fairly easy to identify: a young white male with uncut curly dark hair, a thick charcoal colored beard, wearing rimless spectacles accompanied by an even lighter skinned female, slender, with shoulder length bleached blond hair.

David moved us along making everything easy. Wearing those light sensitive glasses that seem to make even the most innocent person look like a Mafioso, it was apparent from his quiet competence that we were in good hands. After some maneuvering to extricate ourselves from the crowd, we settled into his white Ford Escort sedan.

The warm, damp night rushed against my face as we sped along the Windward Road, through the outskirts of Kingston. A kaleidoscope of strange images tumbled past: goats wearing triangular wooden collars wandering about the street; women squatting along the roadside with baskets of strange fruits and vegetables; barefoot children and near naked toddlers playing in the dirt; a donkey cart filled with freshly cut stalks of sugar cane, bumping along the road ahead while cars, buses and trucks honked impatiently. Only the flicker of candles, the soft yellow glow of kerosene lanterns and the occasional street light illuminated the strange, lively snapshots flashing around me. The little wooden shacks along the roadside crammed with people and animals painted a series of living tableaus that had nothing in common with the Jamaican travel poster in downtown London. Fascinated but exhausted, I relaxed against the backseat and let the tropical night cover me.

~

"He, ha, he, ha," a loud honking sound bellows through the open window. Bright sunlight splashes across the bed. The ceiling fan whirs overhead sounding like a playing card attached to a bicycle wheel making rapid clip clap noise. The honking becomes more insistent, then abruptly stops. I hear the shuffling of slippered feet against the smooth hard tile floor followed by a trickle of water, and someone whispering softly. Closing my eyes, I start to doze again.

Then a high-pitched piercing whine circles above me like an electric current racing through a thin wire. My body, neither hot nor cold, feels pleasantly warm under the lite white sheet. I am waking up in Jamaica!

"Can it be true?" I think as excitement begins to overtake the sleepiness. "What are all these strange sounds?" Now, I must get up and behave like a detective.

In the carport, Granny Ruby pads around a little self made botanical garden of potted tropical plants kept there instead of a car. As she pours water from a small faded red watering can, she speaks quietly to each and every plant.

"Morning, m'love," she greets me. "Did you sleep well?"

"Yes, yes," I affirm, "but what was that loud honking sound in the garden?"

"Oh, that's Mr. Ed, the donkey. He visits every morning and evening braying for Stanton to give him bananas, carrots, or cho cho."

I look down the side garden into the yard where Robert's grandfather, Stanton, his startling white hair glinting in the morning light, is scattering fine seeds to a flock of wild blue and emerald green parakeets that hover around a small mango tree.

"Stanton likes to feed Mr. Ed and the birds every morning before he takes his breakfast," Ruby comments.

"And what about the high-pitched whine I was hearing in the bedroom?"

"Hum, high-pitched whine?" Ruby looks at me quizzically through the small box shaped glasses perched on her prominent nose. The family resemblances passed down the generations from Granny Ruby to Billy her first son and then onto Robert, Billy's first son, are striking. Of course the sizes are different. Ruby can hardly be five feet tall. However, she has the same, broad, squarish shoulders, prominent Jewish nose, and big cheeks, which give her face a warm, happy look.

"Oh, that's a mosquito trying to Kamikaze dive you," a voice interrupts from behind us. It's Robert.

And so our first day in Jamaica begins with lots of questions over a breakfast of long, thinly sliced, orange pieces of "pawpaw" –papaya— dressed with a squeeze of fresh lime juice, accompanied by hot tea and corn flakes.

# THE ALLIGATOR'S TOOTH

By early afternoon, we are sitting on the veranda sipping tea with condensed milk, a thick, syrupy combination of milk and sugar packaged in a child sized tin. Thora and Suzie have joined us. I dunk the "Shirley" biscuits—shortbread cookies— into the tea. They dissolve, soft and soggy in my mouth. The veranda where we sit feels like a little jail because it is enclosed by iron bars, "grills" as Ruby calls them. The door opening into the garden is always locked. There's a pooie tree with delicate pink pompom flowers in the front garden surrounded by impatience plants shouting at us with their bright red, magenta and orange flowers. Spindly poinsettia bushes alternating with leafy uphobia run along the driveway from the carport to the front gate, also locked.

"You'll see, they will look so pretty come December, the red poinsettia with the white euphorbia blooms together," Ruby tells me.

Thora is Robert's second cousin, once removed. What is a second cousin once removed? Thora explains that her mother and Granny Ruby's mother were sisters. That makes Thora and Robert's father, Billie, first cousins. Taking this a bit further, we figure out that Robert and Thora are second cousins once removed. The once removed seems to be an intergenerational thing: Thora comes from Robert's parents' generation, making her "once removed" from our generation! The explanation seems a bit too confusing to really understand, especially if you don't actually know some of the people involved. Suzie, Thora's seventeen-year-old daughter (who is Robert's straight up second cousin with no removals involved) is a near carbon copy of her mother: both have attractive, Latin faces framed by ample dark hair, punctuated with fiery eyes and long V-shaped noses. I am immediately struck by their extraordinary friendliness; their broad, easy to rouse senses of humor and their eagerness to draw us into "the Jamaican family".

Thora begins to regale us with stories while the tea steams in the white porcelain cups. She has a fang-like incisor that is particularly prominent when she laughs which occurs frequently.

"Did Ruby tell you about the alligator's tooth, yet?"

"No, not yet. Ruby please tell us." I beg. Just one day old to Jamaica, I am dying to learn everything as quickly as possible.

~

Before beginning the story, Ruby comments, "The rain soon come."

Together, we look out at the dark curtain of clouds being drawn across the sky. Ruby's stubby, white legs dangle from the aluminum lounge chair, too short to reach the cream colored tiles flecked with gold, terra cotta, and brown that stretch side to side across the veranda floor.

Then Thora, not Granny Ruby, starts the tale while the rest of us continue to sip our tea. As I dip another "Shirley" biscuit into the hot tea, pieces of shortbread begin to disappear in the milky liquid beneath its opaque surface.

"The alligator story begins with Cyril, one of Ruby's great uncles. Together with his brother Manny, Cyril decided to seek his fortune in Greytown on the Caribbean coast of Nicaragua. The year was 1850. The California Gold Rush attracted eager fortune hunters from across the world. People wanted to get to San Francisco as quickly as possible so they could trek to the gold packed foothills of northern California with one objective in mind: to get rich as quickly as possible.

Uncle Manny knew Sir Charles Grey, the British Governor General of Jamaica, for whom Greytown, Nicaragua was named. Sir Charles told him that there was a lot of money to be made in Greytown off the gold seekers who traveled up the river San Juan del Norte with the intent of reaching the Pacific coast of Central America. There they hoped to find boat transportation north to San Francisco. Uncle Manny persuaded his younger brother Cyril to sail with him from Kingston across the Caribbean and down the coast of Central America to Greytown. October of 1850, just after hurricane season ended, the two brothers left Jamaica to seek their fortune in Greytown.

The Greytown they found was a sleepy village where the muddy Rio San Juan del Norte gushed into the glittering blue Caribbean Sea, and lots of "cayman" (alligators) live along the river. Uncles Manny and Cyril, however, weren't thinking about alligators. They were focused on opening a lumber business to fuel the building boom in Greytown.

In a few months, Granny Ruby's family in Jamaica received news that Cyril and Manny had arrived safely in Greytown, and, that they had started their lumber business. Cyril promised to send for his wife and their three young children just as soon as he had built a proper house and the business was making money. Then a silent pall stretched across the Caribbean separating the two men from their families and friends in Jamaica.

More than five years passed before news of Cyril and Manny reached Jamaica again. The news came in a limp brown envelope that bulged with a hard, finger-sized object inside. Friday evening after Shabbat dinner, an anxious family gathered in the parlor of the Kingston Hotel operated by David, Cyril and Manny's oldest brother. A hush fell over the family as David drew the long silver blade of his knife across the crumpled edge of the envelope.

A smooth white tooth the size of a man's finger with a gold band pushed tightly around it dropped from the envelope. In unison, everyone present drew in a terrified breath. Uncle David pulled a sheet of yellowing paper from the envelope. Beginning to read silently, he shook his head with dismay, stopping again and again to grasp at his bearded chin.

"Read it, n' mon," the group started grumbling. "Read de letter!"

"Hold onto your seats now," Uncle David cautioned as he began...

"To our most dear family in Kingston," the words slipped from his tightly pursed lips falling into his lap like lead pellets.

"I write to you with great sadness after so many years have passed since Cyril and I left Kingston much has transpired. We came to Greytown with great hopes of making our fortunes. We found the place to be barely a shadow of Kingston. Yet many people from Europe and the United States are passing through on their way to or from San Francisco with the desire of finding gold, or having found it, of returning to their families with some fortune.

Greytown has grown rapidly since our ship put down anchor over five years ago. Cyril and I joined efforts to establish a lumber business because so many hotels and guesthouses were being built along the bank of the river San Juan. We struggled to make the business grow. The Indians here do not want to work; instead they fish and pick fruits for food. Now many black men from Jamaica have come to work. We hire them to fell trees and to help with the hauling to our mill and also with the sawing and drying of the wood.

It took two years just to get the business established and build a small house at the river's edge. Due to flooding during the rainy season, the house sits on top of stilts like the long thin legs of a flamingo. Shortly after we came here, I took a wife, Mioca. She is a brown skinned Indian woman from a tribe the locals call the Mosquitos. Then our first child, Manrica, a lively girl, was born. Now we also have little Cyril, named after his uncle, and Carita who is still a baby sleeping with my wife in the hammock.

Cyril took a great liking to my children, possibly because he missed his own dear ones so very much. When "Rica" could barely walk Cyril began taking her with him each morning to the river's edge to bathe. Rica delights in the water and loved accompanying her uncle Cyril to the river before the sun heats the air to the temperature of tepid tea. Every morning while Mioca prepared the breakfast, Cyril and little Rica would go for their morning river bath.

As you well remember, Cyril was a great swimmer and water lover. With his strong arms, he could easily swim across the San Juan and back as fast as any man I know, even the Indians, who are accustomed to swimming the river since they were babies. As was his custom, one Tuesday morning after Cyril bathed with Rica in the muddy shallows, he struck out into the current for a swim. Rica stood on the bank watching him.

Then as Rica could best tell us, for she was barely four years when all this happened, Uncle Cyril began screaming for help. "Rica, run, call you daddy, the alligator catch me leg. Help! Run Rica, run!!!"

By the time Rica fetched us, my dear brother Cyril had disappeared into the river without a sign. I practically went mad thinking of Cyril being dragged down by the alligator. Shouting and crazed, I called together a group of men to help me search the river with some hope of saving my brother. We trolled the banks for hours but could not find him.

Come afternoon, hope of saving Cyril had left me. Yet I wanted to continue to search for him. Others gave up, saying it would be no use, especially if the alligator had taken Cyril. You see, the alligator drowns its prey, takes it to an underwater lair and then feeds on the decaying flesh. But still, I wouldn't give up without knowing whether or not this was Cyril's fate.

Every day for several weeks I scoured the riverbanks for signs of Cyril or the alligator. Then just as I was about to give up my search for lack of results, I spotted an enormous alligator at least thirteen feet in length sunning itself on the river bank, not far from the spot where Cyril was accustomed to take Rica to bathe each morning. I approached quietly in my canoe, eyeing the muddy creature that lay still as a felled log except for the twitching of his bulging eyes.

Close enough to have a good look, I stared at what I saw: There hitched onto one of its enormous teeth was a shred of Cyril's blue bath costume. I knew immediately that this was the alligator that had eaten my brother. A wave of rage so strong spread over me that I almost lost my senses with the desire to attack the wretched reptile with my bare hands. Of course, that would have been pure foolishness. Instead, I paddled quickly to the mill to round up several of the strongest workmen to help me capture the devil. Within less than an hour we had returned to the bank where I encountered the beast.

I will spare you the details of the capture. However, once in our possession, we cut the wicked creature's head from it's rough bark-like body, then slit open its belly. Inside we found nothing save the gold wedding band Cyril wore faithfully since leaving Jamaica. Because alligator is a delicacy in these parts, we butchered the meat. I cut out the tooth to which the shred of Cyril's bath suit was stuck. Together with the gold band, I am sending both in this letter to his dear wife and children in Jamaica as the only mementos remaining of this fine man."

~

Spellbound by the story of the alligator's tooth, I looked down at the china plate where uneaten Shirley biscuits stared up at me. "What happened to the tooth?" I gasped trying to sip the now cold tea.

"I gave the tooth to Ruth. She must have it with her t'ings," Granny Ruby replied.

We all have lapsed into silence, perhaps tired from so much storytelling. Raindrops have begun to pelt down from the black sky: tap, tap, tap like someone pouring a bucket of nails onto the tin roof overhead.

The following week, I asked Aunt Ruth about the tooth. She replied, "Oh, yes, I had the tooth. But I gave it to Kay that the last time she came to Jamaica for a visit.

# PEPPER POT SOUP

It's Saturday around half past noon. Robert and I are sitting on the verandah of 10 Donhead Avenue waiting for Georgie, Thora's husband, to collect us for lunch at their house. Georgie is the manager of the Hagely Park branch of the Bank of Nova Scotia. Bald, thin, and a smoker of menthol cigarettes, like Stanton, Georgie tends toward being taciturn, the opposite of exuberant, extroverted Thora. Nevertheless, he exudes gentle warmth, like embers of a dying fire. Georgie graciously chauffeurs us to the Surridge home on Paddington Terrace. The large, low roofed, white house spreads across a broad lawn edged by croton bushes: the gold dust, the corkscrew and the speckled croton each specially dressed with their bright polished leaves looking like an artist has randomly flecked her paint brushes dipped in gold, yellow and red and then splattered color over their shining leaves. My immediate vorite becomes the corkscrew croton with long curling finger-like leaves.

Saturday lunch begins with soup, Jamaican pepper pot soup, which suits Thora's personality to perfection: hot and spicy.

"I put three scotch bonnet peppers in the soup today, because I know that Robert likes his soup hot!" Thora exclaims.

In the palm of her hand sits a brilliant yellow pepper, shaped like a small, fat, puffy elf's hat.

"Oh, no, Thora, you can't put three scotch bonnets in the soup. It's going to taste like fire," Georgie protests.

Thora laughs. "Only one burst, so it won't be too bad," she teases.

"What do you mean burst?" I ask.

"It's the seeds of the pepper that are really hot and the scotch bonnet is de hottest," Thora croons.

"What else is in the soup?"

"Kale, callalou, okra, pigs' foot, scallion, thyme, salt, black and scotch bonnet peppers for seasoning." The only recognizable ingredients in the lot are salt, black pepper and thyme. So I ask Thora to show me some kale (a green leafy vegetable), callalou (which turns out to be a Jamaican variety of spinach) and the pig's foot, which she dredges up from beneath the furiously boiling surface of the soup.

"Then there are the dumplings," Thora remembers, stirring the large tin pot on the gas cooker.

"See one, now," fishing up a grey-whitish golf ball size mound of cooked flour bobbing around in the thick green broth.

We sit down in a small eating porch area with louvered glass windows that look into the garden populated with mango trees, more croton bushes, and numerous potted plants. This reconfirms my observation that gardening and plants have a privileged place in people's lives here.

The table where we sit has a bright, polished plastic surface and the chairs are aluminum framed with glistening red plastic seat covers. It's the kind of plastic that sticks to your skin if your legs are bare as mine are on this warm Saturday afternoon. The "helper" – a Jamaican euphemism for "the maid"-- emerges from the kitchen to serve the pepper pot soup into wide mouthed, shallow soup bowls, which Thora then carries into the dining area, placing one in front of each of us: Robert, Georgie, Suzie, MG (Suzie's twelve year old brother nick named MG for "Master George") and me. Wet ringlets of steam rise above the bowls.

Securing his soupspoon, Robert submerges it into the fibrous broth, lifting the steaming liquid to his lips. He takes in the soup with a definite gulp.

"Great, it tastes delicious," he squeaks and immediately hiccups violently.

Everyone roars with laughter. About to take a sip from my bowl, I watch and listen as Robert changes his opinion,

"Boy is that soup ever hot!"

"Yes, mon," Georgie adds, "It's hot like fire and even hotter like pepper."

A new way of thinking about heat blossoms in my mind at that moment. "Hot like pepper," yes that's the way to describe the chicken curry we ate at a Jamaican friend's house in London last year.

"Choa mon, Thora" Georgie says, "You make the soup so hot that no one can drink it."

True enough, none of us could swallow even a spoon full of the liquid. The pepper was so strong that it singed my lips.

Nonetheless, we all kept laughing as Robert continued to hiccup. Then Thora left the table to search for James, the gardener.

"Come here na, James," she called from the open back door. Presently, James, a wire thin man with chiseled "East" Indian features, barefoot, pants rolled to his bony knees, holding a long bladed machete, appeared on the steps.

"Yes, ma'm"

"James, here, would you like to drink some soup?"

"Yes, ma'm," James replied.

Thora poured the soup from our untouched bowls into an empty kitchen pot. She passed the pot to James, who immediately lifted it to his lips taking a long swig of the soup. He smiled at her with satisfaction.

"See na, James likes the soup and can drink it straight down," she testified.

"Yes, but James drinks pure whites straight from the rum bottle, too," Georgie adds.

After the soup, we continued to feast our way through a meal of fricasseed chicken, rice n' peas, roasted breadfruit, cooked green bananas and salad. Lunch concluded, Thora promised to make another pepper pot soup for us soon: the coming version with only one scotch bonnet pepper for seasoning.

Lunch over we move out to the front porch at the edge of the expansive lawn and garden. People walking along the road travel close to garden fences because there are no sidewalks on Paddington Terrace or most Jamaican roads for that matter. A steady stream of higglers parade along the street selling fruits, vegetables, coconuts, and sugar cane. Most call in from the road before stepping into the yard. Jamaicans who live in the Ligunea neighborhood have dogs, big dogs like German shepherds, Doberman pincers, Ridgebacks and the Rottweilers. Anyone entering a yard needs to be cautious if they don't want to be attacked.

A young, bearded, very black man with wild braids sprouting from beneath a red, green, and yellow knitted cap approaches the gate, calling out:

"Ackee, fresh ackee. Do you want any ackee?"

"Come here na, mon," Thora commands. "No bad dogs here, just push de gate."

"Have you seen an ackee yet?" she asks. "Has Ruby cooked you salt fish and ackee?"

Suzie pipes up, "Salt fish and ackee, that's Jamaica's national dish!"

The young man stands motionless at the gate. He begins to approach slowly with caution, a large cardboard box under one arm. The box is filled to the brim with small bright red, pear shaped "fruits". Some have pale yellow thumbs tipped with a shinny black seed hanging from the fat end of the fruit. Ackee needs to have the fleshy yellow fruit and seeds showing to be eaten. Otherwise, the eater could be poisoned. Thora buys a dozen fruits promising to cook salt fish and ackee for us the next day.

The young man, pleased to sell so many, departs mumbling,

"Praise, Jah."

"That's a Rasta man. They smoke a lot of ganja and think that Haile Selaisse is God. They call him 'The Lion of Judah,'" Georgie remarks as the man slips out the gate. It will take some time before I learn more about the history of Rastafarianism, a religion combining ritualistic elements of the Ethiopian Orthodox Church with the back to Africa movement lead by Marcus Garvey in the 1930s. In time it becomes increasingly clear that Rastafarians are somewhat feared and denigrated in Jamaica—that is until Bob Marley, the famous Rastafarian reggae singer gained international acclaim in the 1970s.

"They call us white people 'trenton' because we look like pink pork meat!" Thora comments. Then she continues with a story.

"In 1965, the Jamaican government invited Haile Selaisse, emperor of Ethiopia, to visit Jamaica. Thousands of Rastas came from all over the island to the airport to wait for his arrival. When the plane touched down and taxied in from the runway, them surge out onto the tarmac and surround the plane shouting, 'The Lion of Judah! The Lion of Judah!' Haile Selaisse took one look at all those crazy Rastas and him too frightened to get out of the plane. He waited for nearly one hour before the po-lise come and contain the crowd. Then when him step out of the plane onto the gangway, the crowd took one look at him and started crying, 'Is white man trick, that little mon could never be the Lion of Judah,'

"You known, Haile Selassie, is a little bit of a man, not even five feet tall and almost as light skinned as Georgie!" Thora laughs.

The story of Haile Selassie's visit will be repeated again over the coming years. Because Robert wears a heavy dark beard and lets his hair grow wild and curly, sometimes when he walks in the street, especially in downtown Kingston, people call out, "White Rasta!" The epithet is just another one of the many stereotypes about race and skin color that permeate Jamaica. At times, when I walk around, I hear men say "white girrrl!"

Being "white" is something I haven't thought much about since leaving John Muir where Robert and I attended high school in Pasadena. Even then I didn't have to think very much about it. Although a third of the students at John Muir were African American, there were never more than two or three in any of my classes. And they were the same students who appeared class after class, year after year: Edna Mosley, Carol Foster, Louis Peters and Nick Johnson.

Now I am wondering how these classmates felt? In Jamaica I am highly visible everywhere I go, except for family gatherings. It takes me a while to get used to always being seen. Actually, I never get completely used to it, but I learn not to let it keep me from doing things, meeting people and going places that I want to visit.

# POUND CLOTH

Shortly after the pepper pot soup meal, Thora invited me to go shopping in downtown Kingston. Dilapidated Victorian houses with peeling paint and cracking staircases lined the streets. Skinny dogs were nosing through garbage strewn gutters; men lounged on the street corners and in rum shops. The women, however, seemed to be walking with purpose from one place to the next. Little girls wearing school uniforms: navy blue cotton pinafores with white blouses, their hair plaited in neat braids decorated with large floppy blue and red ribbons skipped to school. Boys wearing khaki shorts with matching shirts moved in dribbles along the littered sidewalks.

We passed "Parade", a large park with lots of buses surrounding it, then headed down Kings Street, to the main shopping thoroughfare. Kings Street has an excess of shops selling pound cloth

Everywhere, I look I see cloth: inside the shops, in the windows, outside the shops along the sidewalk tables are piled with bolts of material or jumbled with loose pieces of fabric.

Thora encouraged me "to buy some cloth and have a dress made,"

"I have a dress maker in Ligunea Plaza, who sews real nice. She can make anything you want."

I like cloth and I know how to sew, but I have never been to a dressmaker. So we spend quite a bit of time browsing through the materials. Finally, I decide on two fabrics: a heavy lime green, cotton sailcloth decorated with bright orange and yellow vines and a softer blue cotton. I imagine two sundresses, both with spaghetti straps to make me feel more tropical.

Thora finds a sales clerk to help measure and cut the cloth. The woman looks to be in her forties. She wears heavy black rimmed glasses, has a pleasant smile and medium "brown skin". I am just becoming familiar with all the Jamaican skin gradations based on the degree of mixture between African and European heritage. In addition to "brown skin", which looks like café au lait, there is red skinned, a bright amber, mustee-one, a light brown, and even mustaphino, nearly white. All this emphasis on skin color is new to me. Growing up in California, my historical knowledge of slavery was scant. In terms of daily life during my childhood, people were either on the black or white side of the color line. While the subtleties of race and color that permeate Jamaica are new, they reveal themselves with surprisingly alacrity.

Thora appears to know the sales lady already and addresses her as "Miss Lyons".

With our shopping completed, we walk down Kings Street looking for a place to sit and eat. Eventually we find a simple restaurant serving stew beef, rice'n peas; yam and potato. Over lunch, Suzie prods Thora to tell me the story of Miss Lyons.

Laughing gaily, Thora recounts the details of another shopping expedition for pound cloth. Pound cloth is cheap fabric sold by weight rather than length. Apparently, US textile manufacturers habitually dump unsold bulk textiles in Jamaica and other parts of the Caribbean at very low prices. On a previous shopping expedition after the purchases were tallied Thora asked the sales woman,

"Can I pay by cheque, m'love?"

"Certainly, ma'ma, but first I must get de okay of my supervisor."

"Yes, of course. What's your name, m'dear?"

"I am Agatha Lyons, ma'm."

"Lyons, why that was my maiden name!" Thora exclaimed. "Where you com' from?"

"I com' from country, Port Maria way."

"I com' from Port Maria me-self. I belong to Judge Lyons's family."

"Judge Lyons?! Well ma'm, him my pappy!"

Thora laughs uproariously as I imagine she did when the conversation was taking place. "That would make us half sistas, Miss Lyons. You must be one of my dada's outside chil'ren!"

"I suspect it's so, ma'm, because me pappy live in big white wood house in de center of Port Maria. Him come to visit me mother and me from time to time, but him never stay so."

30

Thus Thora discovered her half sister working at the pound cloth store in downtown Kingston. Apparently, this is a big joke in her family. I am really struck by the good humor that surrounds the story. I am also wondering if Miss Lyons and her family see it through the same funny bone lens?

# FAMILY ROOTS

**M'** love, I wonder how Stanton's is getting through the day?" Stanton, who at seventy-three, still rises at six o'clock each week day morning, dresses in a clean, pressed, white shirt, then listens to radio broadcast of the BBC World Service news at 8 am before heading off to work in the accounts department of Marzouka's appliance store in central Kingston. Granny Ruby, however, stays at home as she has always done.

Her question about Stanton is just a way to make conversation and pass the time. I have learned that she doesn't expect an answer. "Sweet" and "naïve" are the adjectives the family uses to describe Granny Ruby, also, seventy-three years old. Both she and Stanton were born in 1895. By watching and listening to her over the next few weeks, certain aspects of life in Jamaica reveal themselves.

Quickly I learn not set a place at the dining table for the amiable, chocolate skinned Florence, who prepares the midday meal, washes the clothes and cleans the house. Florence must eat lunch on the back porch from her own special plate and cutlery while we sit at the large mahogany dining table using the family china. My own working mother hired a once a week cleaning person while I was in high school. The cleaner, a quiet Japanese woman, arrived and departed while the family was out to work and school. Here in Jamaica, "helpers" seem to always be around. The business of having servants to wait on one at home is a strange and yet to become comfortable circumstance.

Also, I learn that Ruby wants to keep the wrought iron gate of the grilled veranda locked at all times. We live in a reverse jail: one that remains locked from the inside out. This preoccupation with "security" belies the gracious, hospitable lifestyle of well-to-do Jamaicans. Within a very short time, the sociologist in me attributes this preoccupation to the obvious differences between a relatively small group of "haves" and the large group of "have nots" who together inhabit this tropical " paradise".

Family members inform us that the "have nots" who live in Kingston slum neighborhoods like Trench Town and Jones Town have televisions in their waterless shanties, while others even have cars parked around the corner from the communal yards where families live four persons to one room! Clearly it's not just smooth sailing in paradise.

Riots in downtown Kingston preceded our arrival by just a few days. Sparked by the government's refusal to allow Dr. Walter Rodney, a

Guyanese history professor at the University of the West Indies' Jamaica campus, re-enter the country upon his return from a conference in Montreal signaled deep feelings of discord. The decision to ban Rodney from ever returning to the island because of his advocacy for the working poor provoked rioting costing the lives of several people and causing millions of dollars in damages.

Still this new life in Jamaica continues to overwhelm me with "the exotic". The abundant flora and fauna constitute part of the wonder of living in Jamaica. Almost immediately, as if they are relatives, Granny Ruby introduces me to the lush plants that spring everywhere voluntarily on any open patch of ground. In her garden, I have already personally met a small mango tree, a beautiful pink pooie tree, hundreds of potted plants in the car port and the euphorbia and poinsettia bushes soon to bloom red and white during the Christmas season.

Exotic fruits like the O'Tahiti apple (a small pear shaped, blood red fruit with cottony white semi sweet insides), the star apple (its smooth tan skin covering a royal purple flesh with a white star design inside), the bumpy sweet and sour sops, the guinep, the Bombay mango, the "Julie" mango, the hayden mango, the number eleven mango abound in the open air market at Papine. Here shoppers bargain with the broad faced higgler women wearing red and yellow gingham dresses, their heads wrapped in kerchiefs. The higglers bring fruits and vegetables fresh from the country before dawn on Friday mornings returning late on Saturday evening after the market closes. We buy samples of as many fruits as the straw basket will hold to experiment with new tastes daily.

While Granny Ruby moves gently through the day with time for an unplanned visitor or unexpected outing to the market, Stanton does everything with clock-like regularity: feeding the birds, eating breakfast, then sitting by the wood case, vacuum tube, Grundig radio to hear morning news. In the evening after supper at the polished mahogany table, he watches the televised news of the JBC (Jamaica Broadcasting Service) Jamaica's only TV station. Then he sits on the veranda gazing through the iron grillwork out into the dark of night.

"Are you ready for your Complan, Stanton?" Granny Ruby calls out. Complan is a British dietary supplement served as a hot or cold drink. When Stanton replies in the affirmative, that means it's getting close to bedtime.

~

Having family close at hand is a novelty for me. Robert's aunt Ruth lived just a short drive from Ruby and Stanton on Belmont Avenue with Pat DeSouza. As diminutive as Granny Ruby, without the plumpness of age and a fireball of energy, Ruth dropped by Donhead Avenue almost daily to check up on her parents. Like her cousin Thora, Ruth was very chatty. But unlike Thora, she seemed to always be on the run to get something done. In that way, Ruth didn't seem so very Jamaican. Jamaican she was, however, born, raised and still resident in the island unlike her two brothers Billie and Walter.

Billie, Robert's father, had been the first Girling to leave Jamaica in 1948. Pressured by Helen, his young wife to immigrate to California where her brother had already settled in the early 1940s, he was constantly on the look out for an opportunity to leave the island.

Emigrating to the States from Jamaica has never been especially easy even in the mid-1940s. The US immigration quota system put in place in 1924 allowed only a handful of Jamaicans to emigrate each year. This waiting list might delay departure for many years. Jamaicans who applied often described themselves as waiting "to be called" by the American embassy. When Billie was offered a job in Bahrain by Pan American Airlines, the company he worked for in the field of telecommunications, Helen rejected the opportunity out of hand. Shortly after, when an opportunity to move to Barbados working in the Eastern Caribbean showed up, the young family quickly decided to take it. The Bajan quota, although much smaller than Jamaica's, had few applicants. Since all the English-speaking islands in the Caribbean were still colonies of Britain, it was easy for locals of one island to move to another.

Meanwhile, Ruth's younger sibling, Walter, who worked with British Overseas Airways, was transferred to Port-of-Spain and remained in Trinidad for many years before eventually settling in England. Billie used to refer to him, as "The Air Vice-Marshall".

This left Ruth on hand to keep an eagle's eye on her aging parents. At times, I felt as if our presence at Donhead Avenue had disrupted a delicate interplay of distant family dynamics. With her brothers gone abroad, Ruth was definitely in charge and enjoyed being so. She had morphed from being sandwiched in the middle, to being like a cherished only child without any competition or interference from her older or young brother.

Ruth both tolerated us and reached out to draw us into her own little Jamaican nest. Making that nest must have been something of a struggle. Hers was a story I had not heard either in California or in England. Like Robert's silence around Anna Kay, I knew little of Ruth before arriving in Kingston.

In fact, the years Anna Kay spent with Robert's family in Altadena were a result of a story the family did not choose to reveal. That story involved the divorce of Ruth from Desmond Silvera, who was part of the enclave, Jamaican Jewish community.

When the marriage with Desmond dissolved, Ruth, like most white Jamaican women of her generation, had neither preparation nor experience for work. While the details of the divorce did not seem to be particularly novel, the results were. Anna Kay was moved to Altadena at age twelve to live with her Uncle Billie and Aunt Helen, while her older brother, David stayed in Jamaica long enough to finish secondary school and then went to England to study engineering. During those years, Ruth re-constituted her life.

By 1968, she was living with Pat DeSouza, another white, Jamaican Jew on Belmont Road at the edge of New Kingston. Pat inherited his family home, an ample rambling wooden house on a sizeable compound of land. The property, shaded by a tall overhang of aged mango trees ran deep. Behind the house was a low slung stretch of building, probably once maids' or maybe even slaves' quarters that Pat had converted into facilities for a small, private primary school he ran. Children whose parents could afford to pay something for their education attended his school. Ruth was there to assist him in every way possible with running the school.

Ruth and Pat shared a passion for their religious heritage, something neither Robert nor I knew much about. From our arrival in Kingston, Ruth issued a standing invitation for Friday night dinner. I recall arriving for the first time at dusk. Both Pat and Ruth were still working in a small office behind the house adjacent to the school building. Pat, a balding, rotund man, in his forties, was occupied with penning, by hand, graduation diplomas for the students of Wolmer's Boys School. With an exceptional talent for calligraphy, Pat's skills were in constant demand. His script could be found on several Jamaican postage stamps.

In anticipation of Shabbat – the Jewish Sabbath – which would begin at sundown, Pat wore a white satin prayer shawl across his broad shoulders. I had no idea about the significance of the shawl, nor did anyone bother to explain. Moreover, everything that happened that evening and any other Friday evening we visited was taken for granted.

Shabbat dinner had its fixed elements: 'cheese cake', the Jamaican version of macaroni and cheese; rice 'n' peas, which had already become a well loved and familiar staple at almost every lunch or dinner; a roast of lamb or beef with gravy and wine, Manoschevitz's wine, that is. The serving of Manoschevitz always gave me the giggles when I caught a glimpse of Robert rolling his eyes. After all weren't we wine sophisticates from California?

Of course, there were other essentials that must have been part of the evening like the obligatory kippah on the men's heads; the breaking of bread, along with prayers in Hebrew that we didn't understand. The lighting of candles always added a lovely touch to the evening.

During Shabbat dinner I felt doubly foreign: not Jamaican and not Jewish. Neither of these sensations, however, was unpleasant. Rather, both felt like being in an interesting maze with surprises at every intersection. Somewhat of a puzzle, however, was that Robert had been raised in a devout Christian Science family when all of his Jamaican relatives were Jewish. That was another story and one which would not be told for many years to come.

From left to right: Anna Kay Newman, Stanton
Girling, Ruby Girling holding David Newman, and
Ruth Silvera

# MEETING THE
# GOVERNMENT OF
# JAMAICA

Two weeks had passed since our arrival from England. The weather and luxuriant tropical flora still seduce me. The pace of daily life feels like a foxtrot that starts, stops then resumes moving slowly around a small dance floor, basically going nowhere. At least that seems to be the life of Granny Ruby: watering her potted plants , supervising Florence, making tea for us to sip together on the tiny grilled veranda. Certain novelties are gradually becoming familiar. For instance, the sticky, sweet off-white condensed milk which drips like heavy sap from a small slit made near the rim of the unrefrigerated tin into the bottom of Granny Ruby's porcelain teacup. Also, the tropical afternoon "showers" that sound like a platoon of snare drummers hammering on the corrugated tin roof.

Other patterns evoke resistance to being normalized. Things like getting used to the ways in which the "help" is treated or talked about and the self imposed restrictions on the movement of white people living here. White people don't walk anywhere or even use the JOS (Jamaica Omnibus Service). They "must" move around in cars or taxis. But Ruby and Stanton don't have a car which together with the grilled veranda make life at 10 Donhead confining. Occasionally to combat the caged feeling, I take off on foot just around the neighborhood or head for the Ligunea Shopping Plaza only a ten minute walk up the Hope Road. They must have thought that I was crazy!

Already this stay in Jamaica has taken on the quality of being something more than a brief interlude. We have come here to live and to work. We must begin paying off the Barclay's advance on our one-way airline tickets. Robert wants to work with the Jamaican government as an economist. He arranges an interview for Thursday morning, ten days after we have arrived.

The last Thursday, October 1968, he returns to 10 Donhead Avenue just before lunchtime, triumphant. He's been offered a job as an economist with the Government of Jamaican's Central Planning Agency attached to the Ministry of Finance.

"When do you start?" I query.

"Monday! And you better go down to the Services Commission to meet with Mr. A.B. Smith. I told him that you are a sociologist. He wants to meet you."

Later in the afternoon following lunch, feeling full to the brim with cho-cho stuffed with minced meat seasoned with scallion, salt, pepper and several dashes of Angostura Bitters, kept company by rice, sweet potato and well cooked carrots  looking like fat thumbs, I try to put through a call to the Services Commission which is the personnel division of the Government of Jamaica. Completing the telephone call is an exercise in patience.

At times when I pick up the receiver, there's no dial tone. Other times, there is the immediate beep, beep, beep of a busy signal without having dialed a single number. When a call actually goes through, it may ring, ring and ring without answer. However, by half past three, I have connected with a secretary at the Services Commission who tells me that she will speak with Mr. Smith and return my call. Late Friday, she finally rings back to inform me that Mr. Smith would like to meet the following Wednesday afternoon.

~

To this day, the appointment with Mr. A.B. Smith remains memorable. First because the Services Commission was situated in what Kingstonians refer to as "Race Course." Race Course, once a horse racetrack, is now an immense open, neglected park area. On its northern boundary sits Wolmers' Boys School, a private preparatory school where Billie, Robert's father, went to school until he was fourteen. Also inside the perimeter of Race Course is Mico Teachers' College a training facility for primary school teachers.

Located on the east side of Race Course is the Services Commission across the road from the Ministry of Finance. On the southern perimeter of the course is the Ministry of Education, and the Ministry of Trade and Industry. These new buildings for a new nation, born August 6, 1962 contrast abruptly with the Services Commission installed in an elegant old colonial home.

Wide shaded verandas ring the building constructed completely from local hardwoods. The desks, which have been placed in the dark, cool entrance, are occupied by a receptionist and several clerks. A ceiling fan rotates briskly creating a medium pitched whir overhead. The receptionist motions me to sit down in a straight-backed wooden chair and wait while the sharp clicking of her high heels on the hardwood floor disappear through the closed door just behind her desk. Presently she returns pointing towards the half opened door.

Stepping into the large, rectangle sanctum, all windows covered with heavy beige curtains, the din of two air conditioners created the sensation of being inside the hold of a cargo plane during flight. Seated behind an immense desk with every millimeter of surface area covered by stacks of pale blue legal-sized file folders sits Mr. A.B. Smith. The folders spread from the desk onto the scuffed hardwood floor. From behind the mountains of folders, Mr. Smith rises, stiff and formal. He towers above me, well over six feet. His skin is very pale; I don't think he has seen the tropical sun in decades. His nose somewhat broad across the nostrils, his lips curled tightly inward and his gray brown eyes narrow as they meet mine.

"Well Mrs. Girling, I understand that you have recently received your Masters' degree in sociology from the University of Essex," his words trot like a well trained show horse and his accent is clipped rather than the soft, pillowy Jamaican I am now growing accustomed to hear.

"Yes..." but before I can say anything else, he continues. "Do you know anything about statistics?" he asks imperiously.

"Statistics?" This is not the opening question I anticipated. "Statistics, yes, I've studied statistics."

"Good. We have a position for an educational planner in the new planning unit of the Ministry of Education. Any applicant for that position must know about statistics. Shall I arrange an interview with the unit director, Mr. Keith Taylor who has recently returned from UNESCO in Paris?"

"Yes, please," I reply without the slightest hesitation, although I have no understanding of exactly what an educational planner might be expected to do, nor what an educational planning unit is, for that matter. Nor, at that moment, do I know what the acronym "UNESCO" (the United Nations Education, Social and Cultural Organization) signifies. So my "yes, please" covers an immense amount of territory yet to be explored .

"We can offer you, one thousand one hundred pounds salary per annum (approximately $2200 US) at the Assistant Secretary level. Civil servants are entitled to one month holiday during their first five years of service. Ministry hours are 8:30 to 4:30 with one hour for lunch Mondays through Fridays and half days on Saturday," Mr. Smith continued.

"I will arrange for you to meet Mr. Taylor at the Ministry as soon as possible. The receptionist will call you." A.B. Smith concluded by raising his eyebrows as if to indicate that I should rise and leave him to the sea of file folders threatening to drown him in this shuttered, air-conditioned sanctum.

Feeling an odd mixture of satisfaction, confusion and curiosity, I stand up and utter a grateful, "Thank you very much."

"You got the job," Robert says as we walk out into the afternoon sun looking for a JOS bus to take us back up to Ligunea. He has accompanied me and seems to be a more confident interpreter of the situation than am I.

Now, so many decades later, I wonder how I might have appeared to A.B. Smith: A slim, blonde, hazel-eyed woman of twenty-three who probably looked more like eighteen wearing a Twiggy length mini dress. He would have heard a pronounced American accent, that is if he had allowed me to speak. Why did he offer me the job so readily? This question would have to wait for more than a decade to find a plausible answer.

~

November 15, 1968, it's early morning and I hear Grandma Ruby pattering around in the carport watering the potted plants. Mr. Ed has just started to bray for carrots at the back fence, while the parakeets form a high-pitched chirping chorus in the yard. This will be my first day of work, at a real job. Physically I want to ready myself by carefully brushing my long straight hair back from my face then hooking it neatly behind my ears. I must fleck a bit of mascara on my pale lashes and choose a comfortable dress reaching just to my knees. Finally I need to identify a pair of low heeled sandals for my feet. Mentally, I have been preparing for this since I was a child, always paying attention in school, always trying to do my best with every assigned task.

Anticipation spreads through me over breakfast. The prospect of working in the field of education stirs excitement. Being part of the new government of Jamaica seems promising. Even though I don't have a clue about what I will be expected to do, I'm eager to put my mind and energy to any task at hand.

We arrange to get a lift with a colleague who drives Stanton to his work in downtown Kingston. Punctually, just as the BBC World Service finishes the morning broadcast, the colleague beeps at the front garden gate. Robert and I climb into the backseat. Stanton takes his place in the front passenger seat. He places his hand atop the full, abundance of white hair he wants to keep carefully in place as the winds rushes to ruffle away the neatness. His cool blue eyes belie a demeanor that is more characteristically British than Jamaican. And as I have learned, his parents did immigrate from Ipswitch, England to Jamaica in the late 1800s.

As our journey dowtown begins the warm morning air rushes through the open windows. Occasionally Stanton raises a hand placing it on his head trying to keep the breeze from ruffling his neatly brushed coiffeur.

Everything in Jamaica still has the flavor of a new adventure, even the ride to the Ministry of Education. We leave Ligunea, picking up Old Hope Road that skirts the National Stadium, then head down Upper Park Camp Road. The traffic slows to a crawl as we pass the Kingston Library and the headquarters of the Jamaica Defense Force inching our way into the Cross Roads area. The entire trip from Donhead Avenue in Ligunea to the Ministry only takes about ten minutes and it is filled with colorful little scenes:

Smartly uniformed mounted police riding a pair of chestnut geldings, their coats glistening in the morning sunlight, weave in and out of the traffic. Along the roadside, children walk hand in hand, girls with bright red and blue ribbons in their tight braids, boys jostling each other in khaki shorts and matching shirts occasionally breaking rank and threatening to spill into the road. As we approach Cross Roads, another uniformed policeman stands stiffly elevated on a pedestal in the midst of the traffic. Dressed like a storybook officer in starched navy blue trousers with a red stripe on the outside of each pant leg, a visored hat pulled low over his face, eyes hidden behind dark glasses, he directs the traffic with his arms as if they were a mechanical signal. Malnourished dogs stray in and out among the crawling vehicles, while a cart man pushes his hand made vehicle loaded with green coconuts and long stalks of sugarcane along the roadside.

We arrive at exactly 8:24 in front of the Ministry of Education, an imposing six-story building. I note parking spaces marked "Minister," "Vice Minister," "Permanent Secretary," "Chief Education Officer," others labeled "EO" and "PAS." From a distance, the Ministry looked formal and modern. As soon as I walk into the open air lobby, a large clutch of people crowd around to enter one of the two small elevators. Some look like Ministry employees arriving to work; others I come to recognize as part of the constant flow of citizens, usually mothers, aunties, and grandmothers. They make pilgrimages to the Ministry from everywhere across the island including the most distant and inaccessible parishes like Westmoreland, Manchester and Portland seeking favors of the Minister of Education.

If I wait to get into one of the elevators, I will certainly be late for my first day of work. So, from this day forward, I decide to climb the cement stairway up six levels to the educational planning unit on the top floor, sandwiched between the library and the Statistics Division. Reaching floor six, I peer through open spaces in the decorative cement blocks that form the southern exterior of the building. The Kingston plain slips away towards the bright blue harbor protected by the palisades, that long stretch of sandy land, skinnier than a witch's index finger. Mango trees sprout among the rusted corrugated tin roofs like dark green broccoli heads offering shelter from the full tropical sun.

The breezeway and stairs echo with many passing footsteps, especially the staccato clicks of high-heeled sandals worn almost universally by the female staff of the Ministry. The multitude of citizens haunting the breezeways waiting for an audience with the Minister, The Honorable Edwin Allen, or one of his designees, appear to be considerably more humble than even the most junior level clerk or stenographer. Usually their mission focuses on a scholarship, a school transfer, or a request for employment – civil service jobs, as I learn quickly are prized for their stability rather than their salary.

Since 1765, when Jamaica was captured from Spain by England, the British colonial government planted and cultivated a sturdy colonial service (now the Jamaican Civil Service) to administer and protect their interests in this island, larger, more beautiful and more productive than other sugar, banana or spice producers they already held in the Caribbean – places like Barbados and Trinidad, and the "lesser" Antilles of east Caribbean: St. Vincent, Grenada, Antigua, Nevis-St. Kitts, and Dominica. Jamaica quickly became the crown jewel of the "British" West Indies as well as preferred hang out of infamous pirates like Henry Morgan and Long John Silver. The British Empire now ended with the wave of colonial independence movements following World War II, has left a substantial home-grown Government of Jamaica bureaucracy, and I am about to become part of it.

Sandwiched between the statistics division and the library, the educational planning unit was tucked away at the far end of the sixth floor. I peeked through the half open door and saw an expansive room with every inch of wall space, from floor to ceiling, lined with metal shelves. Each shelf overflowed with faded pink or blue legal sized file folders. The words "GOVERNMENT OF JAMAICA" were printed across the upper edge of each folder. Each folder was stuffed with yellowing paper. Wooden desks filled the central space, many piled high with the same bulging file folders. On some desks sat upright, manual Royal typewriters. Staff members were arriving at their posts. The men were dressed neatly in slacks and pressed white shirts— mostly short sleeved. The women wore sundresses, high heeled shoes, their hair straightened in bouffant styles and their faces made-up under powder, rouge, eye shadow and mascara. Many looked to be in their late teens and early twenties. Standing floor fans were scattered around the room like lampposts. Across the expanse of the room, I spotted a short woman wearing a uniform style light blue dress. She carried a tray with large glasses of water. I could tell that it was cold from the sweat streaks running down the sides of each glass.

Wanting to get to my own post promptly, I moved down towards the end of the long corridor. A piece of paper taped to a closed door was hand lettered. It read: Educational Planning Unit. Turning the doorknob, I pushed open the door. The interior looked more like a corridor than an office. Two desks which barely fit into the space were lined one after the other and behind the second desk was another closed door. Both desks were empty. I walked into the office, looked around then approached the closed door and knocked. There was no response. So I knocked again, this time with more force. Still there was no response.

Overcome by a puzzled, "What should I do?" feeling, I walked back into the breezeway looking up and down the hall which ran the length of the Ministry, almost a half block in length. The breezeway was surprisingly quiet; all the hustle and bustle I'd witnessed getting up to the Planning Unit had died down. A morgue-like atmosphere prevailed except for the noise floating up from the city below.

I wheeled around to re-enter the Planning Unit with an entirely irrational hope that someone, ghost-like had been hiding in a corner of the office, would materialize when I again opened the door. Of course, no such supernatural event took place, so I simply sat down in one of the empty chairs to ponder the situation. Fortunately, after what seemed to be a long time, but was only another five minutes, the door popped open and an energetic, slightly disheveled man wearing a wrinkled white guyabera, dark pants, and heavy leather sandals without socks walked into the office. He regarded me quizzically, then said in a friendly, non- Jamaican accent,

"Can I help you?"

When I started to explain my presence, he looked quite surprised, but not the least bit flustered. After listening carefully, he replied,

"Well, Keith Taylor, director of the planning unit isn't here yet. He usually doesn't arrived until around 9:30 because he drops his children at school. I'm Ted: I am attached to the Planning Unit. I am doing my Master's degree in sociology at UWI (he pronounced the acronym as U-EE which I later came to know as the local way of referring to the University of the West Indies). Together with Eric Budlah, I work here in the Planning Unit. However, Mr. Taylor didn't mention anything about your joining us."

While Ted's revelation is disturbing, my curiosity about Ted overcomes the feeling of anxiety.

"Where are you from?" I asked. Ted's accent wasn't Jamaican, English, or American. I suspected that he might be Australian.

"I'm a Kiwi," he announced proudly.

"A Kiwi?"

"Yes, mon (he throws in a little Jamaicanism), "I'm from New Zealand. What about you?"

Just at that moment the door swung open again and another tall man with jet black hair, chiseled features, and a sense of urgency stepped into the office.

"This is Eric," Ted said immediately, "Eric, meet Sherry, she's our new colleague."

Eric looked even more surprised than Ted about the unexpected information. Again, however, his surprise had nothing unpleasant about it.

"Eric's from Trinidad," Ted offered.

"What did they hire you as? " Eric asked in an immediate, direct way.

"An Assistant Education Officer," I replied, unclear why this was important information.

"Well I have a meeting with the Chief Education Officer at 9:00, so see you later. Why don't you sit at my desk while I'm out," he then offered.

Two nice guys and two desks, I reflected.

Ted seemed willing and even eager to chat, so we spent the next forty five minutes getting acquainted. Just before half past nine, the door opened again and a third man, no quite so tall, with a nice looking face, dark eyes, dark skin, neatly dressed in suit pants, a well pressed white shirt with no tie, under a matching suit jacket entered office.

"Ah, this is Mr. Taylor," Ted offered a deferential introduction.

Mr. Taylor nodded my way, uncertainly. He was older than Ted, Eric or me, maybe in his late thirties or early forties.

"Yes, Mrs. Girling, I was expecting you," he stated politely. Well, I think to myself, at least someone knows that I am supposed to be here.

"I've got a meeting with the Minister in just a few minutes. You can share a desk with either Ted or Eric and use the library next door, if you like. We can speak later."

Mr. Taylor did not return to the Planning Office that day. Close to noon, Eric reappeared inviting Ted and me to join him in the lunchroom, also on the sixth floor of the Ministry. I begged off, because Robert had arranged to take me to lunch at Tasty Patty in Cross Roads. He'd been raving about Jamaican patties, a crisply baked pastry filled with seasoned minced meat.

"No problem," Eric replied, "we can do it tomorrow, if you like."

Lunch at Tasty Patty or the ministry lunchroom quickly became a daily routine. This would be an important punctuation point in the long, slow days to follow. Moreover, eating in the lunchroom would be the place where I would meet a fascinating cast of characters pushing well beyond the rim of Robert's extended Jamaican family.

# A CAST OF CHARACTERS

When I accompanied Eric and Ted to the lunchroom the following day, I found a very ample, half empty space, partially occupied with long folding tables and chairs where Ministry employees could purchase a home cooked lunch of rice 'n peas, stewed meat or chicken, roast yam, breadfruit, Irish potato, and maybe a little salad or vegetable. Cheap and totally consonant with the Jamaica palate, the lunchroom was rarely filled and frequented mostly by the professional and administrative staff of the Ministry. The food was prepared by several Jamaican women who secured this simple concession by virtue of their political support for the Jamaica Labour Party currently controlling the government. They were also from the Minister of Education constitutency.

The first person Eric introduced me to was John Residen, another young administrative officer in the MOE like Eric. From the moment I laid eyes on John's wire thin physique, bushy side burns, the nervous twitching fingers that often held a cigarette to his broad upturned lips, I knew there was something special, something wonderfully warm and friendly about John. John was to become an important interlocutor who would include me in a small circle of emerging artists and theatrical people on the Kingston scene. In particular, I got to know Lloyd Record (actor/director) intimately involved with producing the annual Pantomime—a form of Jamaican theatre centered around popular patios culture as well as Lloyd's partner, the impish, irreverent Collin Garlin, a surrealist painter transplanted from Australia to Jamaica.

Lloyd was digging into the complex roots that were Jamaica's. Roots that intertwined a legacy of British education, governance and habits with the historically devalued culture of Africa brought to the island by slaves shipped from the Gold Coast of West Africa across the Atlantic. He belonged to a highly creative group of cultural movers who were gay in an intensely homophobic society. Their talent, however, seemed to protect them as well as eventually earn them national and Caribbean wide acclaim. And I had never before known anyone who was openly gay.

John also knew just about everyone in the MOE from the women who served iced water to the professional and administrative staff right up to the Minister himself. He was especially close to Ross Murray, the Chief Education Officer, who occupied the top professional post in the MOE and had been a classmate of Robert's father at Wolmer's Boys School. It was John who eventually introduced me to

Elizabeth Ramesar, another young Trinidadian with a degree in psychology from Colombia. Elizabeth had come to the MOE shortly before I arrived. She would become a friend, one of the few female friendships I was to develop in Jamaica during the coming years.

Because Elizabeth and I were the only two young female professionals working at the Ministry, we became more closely associated than I did with any of my other colleagues. We didn't see very much of each other at work because Elizabeth was locateded on the second floor with the only high level female professional in the Ministry at the time, Trixie Grant, an educational psychologist, who quickly took Elizabeth under her wing. Elizabeth began inviting me and by extension, Robert, to socialize with her American co-worker friends and a Swedish expert with whom Elizabeth quickly became an item.

"Experts" like these generally spent between two to four years in Jamaica providing "technical assistance" to the MOE on various aspects of education: school design and construction, curriculum development, teacher training and information systems. Hailing from metro-poles like Toronto, London, Los Angeles, Boston, and Stockholm, they all drew large salaries, lived in luxury homes, and drove oversized American cars. The experts were able to afford weekend excursions to hotels on the North Coast. As we began to socialize with this group, I felt quite ambivalent about their privileged status. Their complaints about the "locals" irritated me in the same way that family conversations about "the help" did.

Nonetheless, Elizabeth seemed to have a strong affinity especially for the Americans attached to the Ministry. Now, I can only surmise that

Elizabeth's attraction for the foreigners must partially have had origin in the same uncertainty about her place in Jamaica—an uncertainty that we never spoke about. Personally, I saw her as much more of an insider. Her mother, a medical doctor and a Jamaican of light brown complexion had married a Trinidadian and lived in Port-of-Spain where Elizabeth was born and raised. I am not certain whether the marriage dissolved or Elizabeth's father died. He was never mention. However, Elizabeth left Trinidad to study psychology at Colombia and returned to Jamaica, where her mother had relocated and was in charge of a government-sponsored children's health center. They shared a house on Karachi Avenue, near to the university.

Elizabeth's most striking feature was her waist length, heavy, silk black hair that she often wore loose to great advantage. The mix of East Indian and diluted African heritage revealed itself in an amber brown skin tone, dark eyes, a few freckles on the sides of her nose, thin lips and the ever attention attracting long, straight, hair. Elizabeth's accent was also an odd, unidentifiable concoction of British, American, Trinidadian and Jamaican English. She seemed to be from everywhere at the same time.

Occasionally, there would be an excursion with the "experts" to the north coast or other parts of the island. One Saturday we rose before dawn to drive to Discovery Bay for a snorkeling expedition. The group had identified a local fisherman with a small boat powered by an outboard motor to take us across the wide bay where Columbus is reputed to have first landed in Jamaica. Taking turns being shuttled by boat out to the reef, Robert went in the first group while I came later. Arriving at the reef, others were already jumping into the water. Robert followed suit. I watched him plunge into the deep blue not far from the boat in which I was seated. The boat was still circling round slowly. Suddenly I heard the sound of a dull thud. Then within seconds Robert popped to the surface with blood streaming from his head. He'd collided with propeller of the outboard motor!

There's nothing bloodier than a head wound. Quickly we pulled him into the boat and took off fast across the bay.

"There's a small clinic on the Kaiser bauxite loading premises where we can take him," someone said.

Reaching shore, the boat hull was awash in bloody red water. Hurriedly we drove to the clinic to find a calm, competent Jamaican doctor. He applied pressure to stop the bleeding and then stitched up the wound. Needless to say, that ended the anticipated day's snorkeling before it even began. For the next week Robert wore what looked very much like a pirate' bandage around his forehead. He was roundly teased for engaging in too much swashbuckling on the weekend.

After the Discovery Bay fiasco, we were somewhat surprised to be invited on another snorkeling expedition. This time the diving trip was charted for Pigeon Island off the south coast not far from Old Harbour. The group hired two small outboard fishing launches to take us to the island. Rumor had it that a hotel magnate was trying to buy the island with plans to put a small plane landing strip there for his private use.

The diving was exquisite: calm water from fifteen to thirty feet deep with scattered coral reef and lots of sea life receding below us. Barracuda swam past with their razor sharp teeth; angelfish darted delicately in and out of the coral; lobster crept among the rocks, while eels undulated from the crevices with the under water currents. An abundance of conch living on the sea floor was quickly discovered. The group went wild diving for the conch. When we climbed into the launches for the return trip, more than forty creatures living in their elegant, white shell houses with shinny pink walls had been collected.

"It's too much," I protested. "What are you going to do with all of these? Throw some back into the sea."

"No, no," a chorus of voices responded in unison. "You can make conch soup and then save the shells for decorations."

"But not so many." My objections, however, fell on deaf ears. The launches sped away, hulls filled with conch.

~

Fortunately with John's far flung network of connections, he soon introduced me to the brilliant Ronnie Manderson-Jones. I cannot forget the first time I turned to see Ronnie cross the MOE lunchroom hailing John who was seated across from me. Ronnie, then, with the tall lithe body of a long distance runner, wore a navy, blue double-breasted suit and matching tie. His face, long and sculpted, like an elegant African mask, was shaped by high cheekbones and decorated with arched brows above penetrating eyes, while his lips were edged by a trim moustache which grew into a well kept goatee covering his chin. Actually, I would have expected to see Ronnie walking along a busy sidewalk in London or New York, rather coming to meet John and his friends in the MOE lunchroom.

John was quick to make the appropriate introduction, immediately informing me that Ronnie had just finished his doctorate in international relations at the London School of Economics and returned to work with the Jamaican government.

"Yes, for a moment I thought you were, Mmie, my wife, before I saw your face," Ronnie commented.

He also seemed genuinely interested to know that I had studied sociology in England and that my husband was an economist in the Central Planning Unit. But when we discovered that he and Marlene, his English wife, also lived on Donhead Avenue just a few blocks from us, the friendship was sealed.

"Let me check with Mmie about having you round for a drink Thursday evening," Ronnie quickly initiated. "I'll come by to collect you about half past seven if it's alright."

"Thank you, Robert will be delighted to meet you," I responded. And as I predicted, Robert was. Ronnie, a fantastic, provocative, insightful conversationalist, was expansively interested in just about everything. He was a true intellectual, albeit a conservative one. If ever the saying, "more British than the English," were true, this applied to Ronnie. He had absorbed and mastered the best British colonial education: he could quote from 18th and 19th century English poetry at will; he knew the history of the British empire and their colonial rule in Jamaica without exception because he had earned a first class honors degree in history at the University of the West Indies before taking up a scholarship to study international relations in England.

His ambition was to be a diplomat for the newly independent government of Jamaica. Oddly, however, upon his return from studies abroad, he had been assigned to the Pig Advisory Board's desk at the Ministry of Agriculture. Robert and I occasionally speculated on this anomaly. How could someone as smart and highly qualified be so misallocated professionally?

From our first evening with Ronnie and Marlene we continued to uncover more and more common ground. We were young, professional couples with considerable ambition, all bridge players, and *aficionados* of a good intense discussion about some topic of agreed importance which could be anything from whether or not Jamaica should invite more foreign investment, or join Caricom—the recently formed inter-regional Caribbean trade association or whether or not the current Prime Minister, Hugh Shearer, was doing a good job leading the country. All these commonalities drew us closer together. Moreover, with three of us working for the GOJ (Government of Jamaica) we could easily trade civil service stories, information and policy insights— especially Ronnie and Robert.

We also discovered that Ronnie and Marlene liked weekend day trips to the country of which we organized many. In the course of these excursions, Ronnie revealed himself to be something of an

Indianapolis 500 race car driver. A speedster myself, I still felt terror each time we drove together in his imported, left hand drive BMW on narrow roads behind country buses loaded atop with suitcases, produce and fruits of "higglers" moving in and out of the corporate area on the weekends. Ronnie would first drive right up on the bus' tail then flagrantly begin cursing in Jamaican patios at the lumbering vehicle which continuously belched thick black smoke into our faces. He would honk for the bus to pull over, a useless exercise, because there was never any shoulder on the twisty single lane roads. Then he would momentarily decelerate, pull radically right around the bus without much vision of what might be coming from the opposite direction given his left side driver's position, and jam the accelerator to the floor. Fortunately the car was overpowered for the condition of Jamaican roads. Nevertheless, these were harrowing experiences; so much so that I began to insist with Robert that either we drive or make an excuse to go separately.

When I met Marlene (Ronnie always called her "Mmie") I could see why he might initially have mistaken her for me from the back. She had the same shoulder length blond hair, slight stature, and off white skin color as mine. She was very English, however, without any intention of making herself into a Jamaican wife. She was finishing her doctorate in Caribbean history at the UWI with considerable earnest. Yet, she played the role of a competent housekeeper, neither Ronnie nor Marlene wanted a "helper" in their home, as well as a tranquilizing mate.

As we lived longer in Jamaica and eventually became acquainted with young faculty at the university, it also surprised me that Ronnie had no close friends among them. He was well known because of his sparkling mind and stellar academic performance. However, his relentless, undaunted approach to dialogue could be formidable. Moreover, his views of the world were mostly out of step with the emerging radical perspectives, highly critical of Jamaica's colonial past and any continuity with that history in the present. And as Robert put it, "Ronnie was never one to suffer fools gladly."

Nevertheless we continued to be a well matched foursome during all the years we lived in Jamaica. The friendship even sustained itself after we left Jamaica definitively. When we returned in the 1990s, Ronnie and Marlene had divorced. Ronnie in his characteristically indomitable manner found another wife, a lovely young, high intelligent economist, who like himself did not like "to leave the rock" as many sophisticated Jamaicans were prone to proclaim.

One of the main advantages life in Jamaica afford the very educated professionals, usually "brown skinned", but not always, was protection from the rampant racism they would have to confront when choosing life in North America or Britain. Moreover, the fact was that in this new world of independence, they were the people who were positioned to be at their nation's helm.

# 19  SPATHODIA AVENUE

We lived with Ruby and Stanton at 10 Donhead Avenue until January 1969. This gave us time to get our bearings, to start paying back the loan we took from Barclays Bank to buy our one-way tickets, while settling into our jobs with the Government of Jamaica.

Then more luck came our way. The director of the Central Planning Unit where Robert worked told us that there was a government house becoming available in Mona Heights, which we could rent for only $40 (Jamaican) per month. And, if we would like, we might have furniture and appliances for another $10 monthly.

Jamaica's very first housing track, Mona Heights bordered on the University of the West Indies campus. Although the houses were basically unimaginative square boxes built from concrete blocks topped with flat roofs, most residences had been painted distinctively, their patios expanded for more outdoor living and the gardens prettied up as Jamaicans seem so inclined to do.

Nineteen Spathodia Avenue looked a bit dismal by comparison with many of the other houses on the block. However, the three small bedrooms, living room, dining area, small kitchen and laundry porch added up to more house than we needed. The garden had three mango trees: a Julie, a Bombay, an East Indian along with an ackee tree! This meant that we could have fruit year round.

There was also a little house in the garden— the maid's quarters with a small room and tiny bathroom.

"We could rent it to a student at UWI," was the first thought that came to mind. Not too long after we moved in, Zanobia, a friendly Trinidadian girl studying X-ray technology at the UWI, fulfilled the fantasy.

Magenta bougainvillea hedged the rather barren front yard patchy with Bermuda grass. The interior of 19 Spathodia had been painted steel gray.

"We can fix that with another color," Robert and I agreed quickly. So it was decided, that we would move in the beginning of February.

Thora, with her characteristic generosity, gave us a yellow, orange, and red floral patterned sofa and matching armchair. We put a mattress on the floor of the bedroom that looked out onto the front garden, and used one of the back rooms to store our suitcases, my miniature Singer sewing machine and the Smith Corona portable typewriter. We simply closed the door to the third bedroom. It would eventually have another mattress on the floor for the occasional guests.

Florence, Granny Ruby's helper, agreed to come and do the washing and a bit of cleaning one day each week and Thora offered James' services for the garden.

"We don't need a gardener," was Robert's definitive reply.

Shortly after moving to 19 Spathodia one of the neighbors offered us kittens from a fresh litter. The two adorable tortoise-shell kittens were named Yoni and Cass. We decided to shut them up in the house for the first few days meant keeping all the doors and windows closed. Naturally, this made the house heat up like a big oven during the day. Coming home from work was like stepping into a sauna. Wednesday evening, however, when we walked into the house , there were no little bouncy kittens there to greet us

"Where are they?" We looked everywhere around the house, but no kittens could be found. We were really feeling downhearted. How could they have gotten out?

Robert went out into the garden to search for Yoni and Cass. It was almost dark. From the kitchen where I was preparing dinner, I heard a yelp. Rushing to the garden, expecting to find Robert with one or both of the kittens, I saw him pointing to a dark kitten sized object in the grass. Suddenly, the object leapt into the air.

"It's a toad, " he exclaimed. "I thought it was Cass or Yoni. When I grabbed it, instead it was a big fat toad!" Amused, but still dejected we went inside to eat dinner.

Later in the evening, Thora and George stopped by for a visit. Jamaica is like that. Friends and family just come by your house if they want to see you. Maybe it's because we didn't have a telephone. Even if we did, the telephones often didn't work well. So when you wanted to see someone, you just go look for them at their house.

By the time Thora and Georgie arrived, we had opened the louver windows and the front door to cool off the house. Seated in the linving room chatting a soft scratching sound leaked from inside the sofa.

"Ssssssh, I hear something. Listen, do you hear it?" We're all quiet as mice. Sure enough there was some more scratching. Robert lifted a cushion and peered into the innards of the sofa. Then he reaches down and pulls up a kitten! It was Cass wiggling and meowing in his hand. "Yoni must be in there too!" he exclaimed. We took off the other cushions and eventually found Yoni still trying to hide. Finally, we coaxed her out with a string.

We' were so happy to have our kittens back that we decide not to keep them cooped up inside any more. Pretty soon they both were chasing toads in the garden and scrambling up and down the mango trees.

~

One Sunday we decided to drive our small Ford Anglia out the St. Thomas road to explore the beach belonging to the University of the West Indies. Elizabeth came along bringing with her a friend, Robert Lightbourne, Jr. When there is a junior, a senior has to be lurking somewhere. In Robert Junior 's case, the senior stood out rather than receding in the background, casting a long shadow across his first-born son. Currently, the Minister of Trade and Industry, Lightbourne senior was also known as Mr. 10%. No one, however, could say that about Robert Jr.

A tall angular young man, with a square jaw and uncertain eyes, Robert Jr. was literally jammed into the tiny back area of the Anglia, next to Elizabeth. From there, he managed to conduct a full-blow conversation about his work with the family planning campaign currently underway in Jamaica.

When first meeting Robert Jr., I would have to say that his most distinguishing characteristic was a prominent stutter. He had clearly received coaching for the stutter because when a word got hooked in a loop mid syllable, he simply stopped, held on to the half completed sound and eventually resumed. Initially, I felt tempted to complete the hanging word, but this urge soon dissolved because he had an earnestness about him combined with lots of very intelligent conversation.

During the drive along the narrow two-lane road weaving through open savannah then crossing a wide, dry riverbed, he talked about the government's family planning campaign. I'd seen large billboards depicting a lunging black panther, which advertised the use of condoms. The billboards were curiously pitched to men. In the corporate area, I'd also seen graffiti scrawled across walls, shouting "Birth Control, A Plot to Kill Black People".

I queried Robert Jr. about the government's birth control campaign, wanting to know why it was important.

"Over population is a key contributor to poverty," he replied. "Poor Jamaican women have too many children. They can't afford to take care of the children and neither can the fathers. Jamaica is a very small island with limited resources. We need to control the population, so that there is more for everyone."

"Humm... do you think that by curtailing the population, that the poor will actually get a bigger share of the resources?" I questioned. "And it seems odd to me that the campaign targets men rather than women. Women are the ones who have the babies."

"True, but surveys we've done indicate that women won't insist that men use birth control. We're focusing on the men, trying to encourage them to take responsibility."

By now I'd read a book titled, *Family Structure in Jamaica.*

"But that thinking seems circular to me. Women need access to birth control, education, and jobs to reduce their fertility," I countered. "I've read that Jamaican women get pregnant by different men as an economic survival strategy. Once they have a baby, the baby's father will support them for sometime. When that support dries up, they look for another man to help and often end up pregnant again.

"An article in *Social and Economic Studies* documented how much Jamaican women work. They have one of the highest labour force participation rates of women anywhere in the world. Nearly as many women work as do Jamaican men. But regular, full time, year round jobs are very difficult to find especially for anyone without an education.

Maybe that's why so many Jamaicans want to migrate to England, Canada and the US?" I continued.

"It's quite probable that lack of work contributes to migration. By spotlighting men in the birth control campaign, we hope to change men's attitude about fathering children. Jamaican men want to boast that they have fathered children without assuming responsibility for their children," Robert Jr. added.

"I just don't see how reducing the population will necessarily change the distribution of income or wealth in Jamaica. There needs to be other measures taken to do that. Otherwise, there may be fewer people, but the same proportion will remain poor," Robert interjected from the driver's seat, having been silent until now.

"The issue regarding poverty is central to the country's development. Without policies to reduce poverty, increase employment, and raise productivity, things won't get better. The private sector hasn't done much in this regard. Especially the big multinationals like the bauxite companies and the tourist industry. These sectors take most of the value that is produced in Jamaica out of the country. Meanwhile, agriculture continues to lag. And, as G.Beck wrote in *Persistent Poverty*, without changing the underlying economic structure of the plantation society, Jamaican won't move forward," Robert, the economist, comments.

The conversation notched up in intensity. I decided that it might be a good idea to cool things a bit. After all, we've just met Robert Jr., so maybe it's better not to get into a big brew ha-ha.

"It must be very interesting visiting the family planning clinics around the island," I suggest.

"Yes, it is and the women that I have interviewed really express their satisfaction with the clinics. One young mother I spoke with at a clinic in Annotto Bay said that the clinic was so helpful, before, during, and after the pregnancy, that she decided to name her baby after the clinic.

"So I asked her, 'What is your baby's name, Miss Brown?'

"Me call de pic'ney Antenatal Brown, sir" was her reply.

Just then the road turned north skirting near the fluorescent turquoise shoreline. Dotted along the roadside were little wood stands with a few home picked fruits like the giant, lumpy jackfruit, breadfruit, naseberries, green coconuts and pawpaw for sale to passersby. We all fell into silence under the spell of the lush surroundings. Arriving at the university's beach, we found the parking area full of ginup trees. Picking up the small fruit underfoot, we cracked their brittle green leather skins, then sucked the sweet, mushy white flesh off the hard round seed. The conversation lit up again this time shifting to bauxite and the possible ways Jamaica could earn more revenue from this valued mineral resource.

~

After most of the morning and early afternoon on the palm studded beach, looking much like the travel poster in London which lured us to Jamaica, I felt drowsy from too much tropical sun. As soon as we arrived at 19 Spathodia, I flopped down on the mattress falling instantly asleep in the warm lap of the late afternoon. Awakening to the fading light of dusk, a curious swath of black stretched across the bedroom wall from one of the open louver windows to the other window, just above the bed. Had someone painted a thick black strip across the wall? Finally, managing to rouse myself from sleepiness, I switched on the overhead light. This made scrutinizing the black stripe possible.

"Wow, Robert come here! There are thousands of tiny black ants crawling in through the open window and marching across the wall to the window on the opposite side of the bedroom then disappearing outside again. It looks like an entire colony of ants is moving from one side of our house to the other and taking a short cut through the bedroom! And these are the stinging ants. Get me out of here."

We stood in the doorway watching the moving ant colony. To our surprise, the ants took less than 30 minutes to cross the walls, continuing their journey to a new home on the other side of the garden.

~

At 19 Spathodia, we quickly fell into a comfortable daily rhythm. It's off to work every morning at 8 a.m. after a mango from the yard and some uncooked oatmeal wetted down by evaporated milk and sweetened with a bit of unrefined, large grain, golden brown demerara sugar. We would come home in the evenings and experiment cooking Jamaican recipes, especially spicy ones like curried chicken, and a toned down version of Thora's pepper pot soup. I learned to take extreme care when cutting up peppers. The seeds and oil from inside the brilliant orange scotch bonnet or a red fiery bird pepper can seriously burn ones' fingertips or lips. On more than one occasion this happened as I tried to master the tasty art of Jamaican cuisine.

On the weekends, we explored the island as much as possible. Thora insisted that we visit Port Maria, where she spent her girlhood as the daughter of Judge Lyons. She arranged a family excursion which included stops in Port Maria, Port Antonio and Boston Beach where we swam and ate jerk pork.

In 1968, Boston Beach was the only place in Jamaica to eat jerk. The roasting began in the wee hours, long before the sun rose. Prepared by men, a fire of annotto wood was burned to a bed of glowing coals. The pork meat slathered with a thick paste of chopped peppers, scallion, thyme, garlic, and annotto was then placed between sheets of corrugated zinc atop the fire. The upper layers of zinc were covered again by more coals. The meat cooked slowly to be ready by mid morning when visitors began moving along the road. One of the cooks would cut the fatty pieces of pork, placing them in brown paper together with hard dough bread—a dense, heavy white bread that soaked up the meat juices and helped cool the peppery heat of the jerk seasoning.

On this excursion I saw Monkey Island and Sans Sans beach for the first time. The water, irresistibly blue, seduced us into stopping immediately. We climbed the roadside railing to diving headlong into the warm Caribbean. Swimming across the channel separating Monkey Island from the coast, we reached the mirage like destination. The warm, wet, white sand sparkled with gold flecks.

Covered with coconut palms, the island appeared to be the inspiration for Robert Louis Stevenson's *Treasure Island*. We indulged ourselves in this miraculous beauty by lolling on the beach and digging our toes into the fine gleaming sand. With the taste of salt on my lips, warm water evaporating from my skin while the sun beat down on my face and the sensuous sand oozed beneath my toes, life felt hyper-real. I couldn't quite believe that I was actually here in this island paradise.

~

Florence came each Wednesday to 19 Spathodia. She was sturdy as the trunk of a mahogany tree, rounded as a watermelon, with strong arms and hands that were capable of washing sheets and towels in the rough cement tanks on the back porch. After the washing, rinsing, and wringing out as much water as possible, she would spread the wet laundry helter skelter on every bush around the garden for the hot sun to dry before ironing each piece crisp and clean.

Although we didn't truly need Florence, we quickly came to depend on her. And, she was as dependable as the sunrise or the sunset. Moreover, she proved herself to be unswervingly good natured, with a full laugh, and a thick smile revealing a good set of white teeth. Her voice was sweet and smooth like chocolate syrup in the range of an alto sax constantly chatting in a steady stream of Jamaican patios.

There was nothing obsequious about Florence. She was naturally polite, warm hearted, and pleasant as a cool sip of coconut water on a hot afternoon. Florence arrived by 8 am on Wednesday mornings. The journey from West Kingston involved several bus transfers before she could thread her way through Mona Heights to 19 Spathodia by foot. She made the return trip in the evening as soon as we arrived home from work. Usually, she came to our house looking more like a country woman with her stout body often clothed in a red, yellow and white gingham dress that rode high on her firm protruding belly. Even though her hair was cropped closed to her large, well shaped head, she did not wear a kerchief over it.

Everything about Florence was simple and easy. Born in the country, her parents were farmers as were their parents. She came to work in Kingston when she was just twelve, having completed nearly three years of primary school without fully learning to read or to write.

Thinking back, now, I realize that we knew little about Florence from the beginning and only slightly more after she had worked with us for two years. Florence rarely offered any information about herself, although I discovered over time that she would talk if asked.

Gradually, Florence revealed that she lived in a room with her four year old daughter, Jenny. The room was part of a "yard" somewhere in West Kingston. Weekdays, Jenny went to the Dorothy Lightbourne Children's Center and Clinic not far from the Ministry of Education on the west side of Race Course.

Eventually, Florence told me that she had two older daughters, one who had emigrated to Canada and the other that still lived in the country with her grandparents. Florence also confided that her own dream was "to go foreign" so she could earn more money and make a better life for herself and Jenny.

As part of her plan to go foreign, she belonged to a *susu* which she described as a group of eight women who had formed a kind of savings circle. Every week each woman contributed a day's wage to the *susu* from her earnings. And each week it was a different woman's turn to take the *susu*, meaning that she would have an extra week's wages to do with as she needed. Florence saved her *susu* for that time in the distant future when she would be able to go foreign.

We paid Florence about double the going wage for a day's work. She would wash, dry, and iron the clothes, clean the kitchen and bathroom, sweep and wash the floors throughout the house as well as the front veranda, and prepare something for our dinner after work. She seemed very pleased with the arrangement, and so were we.

Occasionally, when the Children's Center was on holiday, Florence would bring Jenny to 19 Spathodia. Sweet like her mother, Jenny had the same round face, wide spaced eyes and broad noise, although her hair was always carefully plaited and tied with blue and red ribbons and her dressed nicely washed and pressed.

I remember talking with Florence about what would happen with Jenny when she left the island.

"She go stay with me modder in country. She used to stay there when she was lit-all lit-all, but me modder no feed she enuf so me bring she to Kingston."

On July 24, 1969, three days after Neil Armstrong, the United States astronaut, was televised landing on the moon, I asked Florence if she watched the broadcast and what she thought about it.

"No'm me no see it. Me no have television. But me no t'ink it true so. Is (h)oax, it tis. No man can reach de moon, so."

The surprise, which wasn't so much of a surprise if I had thought more carefully about it at the time, was that Florence couldn't imagine a person walking on the moon. To her this seemed absolutely ridiculous and without importance. And to me, as believable as the moon landing was, at that moment I began wondered about the importance of sending people to the moon, when so many were struggling from day to day to feed and clothe themselves and their families. Really did this make any sense at all?

~

One afternoon in early February, we stopped at Ligunea Plaza to do some shopping. Pushing a cart filled with groceries across the parking lot, I spotted Robert standing by our car. Beside him was a young man wearing torn, dirt streaked khaki shorts and a discolored blue t-shirt. His uncut hair stuck out in nappy clumps, and his right forearm dangled lifelessly from the elbow.

Robert told me, "This is Ken. He begged me to give him some money. Then I asked him if he knew how to use a machete, and he says that he does." All the while Robert spoke, Ken stood morosely behind him looking at the ground. His eyes appeared bloodshot and dreamy.

"I'm going to bring him to the house and let him do some gardening for us," Robert continued.

And so, Ken became our "gardener." From the outset, I felt uncomfortable around Ken. His disheveled countenance and wild, unpredictable eyes worried me. I kept thinking, what's he going to do next? Ken did a bit of grass cutting in the front garden then trimmed the overgrown bougainvillea hedge. Robert paid him with instructions to come round in two weeks. However, Ken showed up much sooner, again begging for money.

Not sanguine about Ken showing up unexpectedly, I suggested, "Let's have him come the same day that Florence is here then she can kind of watch him while we're at work."

The following week when we arrived home, Ken had been gardening again. Shortly after he left, a neighbor came by, asking Robert to "please discipline your gardener".

"What do you mean?" Robert inquired.

"Well your gardener took off all his clothes and was cutting the grass naked right here in the front yard. I don't think that's right, especially for the children coming from school," he answered.

"I don't think so either," I concurred, echoing the man. "See, I told you that I think Ken is a bit crazy." Robert laughed, promising to tell Ken to keep his clothes on.

Robert felt sorry for Ken, who told us that he came from Oracabessa on the north coast. He moved to Kingston when he was nineteen. His intention was to look for work, however he couldn't find any. So he started hanging around the Ligunea and Lane plazas, where wealthy Jamaicans do their grocery shopping, to beg for money. One day, he asked some school children for money. When they refused, he followed them to their home. The frightened children ran into their yard. Within minutes their father came out angrily waving a gun and shot Ken in the hand. Ken went to the university hospital for treatment, but never regained use of his hand or forearm. Now, two years later, he's just twenty-one and still begging in the plazas.

I asked Florence what she thought about Ken.

"Him no problem, ma'am. Him just a little spooky an' smoke too much ganja."

Ah yes, that explained the blood shot eyes, they must be ganja eyes.

At Easter time, we took a week's holiday in Negril. Before leaving we reminded Ken that he didn't need to come to garden while we were away. Upon our return, I noticed that Zanobia, our Guyanese student tenant, wasn't in her room in the backyard.

"I wonder where she's gone? It's so strange that she's not here."

Midweek, Zanobia returned just as we were about to eat dinner.

"Where have you been?" we asked.

"Well, I went to stay with a friend last week."

"Why?"

"On Monday, the gardener came round and started knocking on my door. I told him to go away, but he stayed for a long time before leaving. I felt really uncomfortable being here alone, so I went to stay with a friend until you came back."

"Oh my, we're so sorry. And I know what you mean about Ken. I feel uncomfortable around him as well," was my collaboration to her tale.

That ended Ken's gardening career at 19 Spathodia Avenue, Mona Heights. Shortly afterwards, we learned that Ken was a psychiatric patient at the University of the West Indies hospital. When we spotted Ken again at Ligunea Plaza, we gave him some money instead of work.

Left to right:  Chalyn, Sarah Foster-Davis, Lisa Foster-Davis, Georgie Surridge, Steven Taylor, Thora Surridge and Arthur Taylor at San San Beach.

# MORE THAN A BEACH

By early summer 1969, we had settled into Jamaica. Our life was simple and good. By comparison with most Jamaicans, we would be considered really well off. By comparison with our "peers" we live modestly. Occasionally, we ate out at Jing Wah, a Chinese restaurant. Jing Wah's was above a plumbing supply store in Ligunea along the Hope Road. The store, restaurant, and other small shops in the pocket plaza were owned by "Chinee" (Chinese)-Jamaicans.

Like a Chinese restaurant anywhere, Jing Wah had a lighted tropical fish tank, complete with a neon orange castle where a lonely angelfish and an aggressive blue tiger fish swam monotonously in and out of the castle door. The polished black surfaces of the dining tables reflected your face like dark mirrors while dusty red lanterns with gold tassels dangled from the ceiling. Dreamy watercolor pictures of mountain scenes captioned with brushed Chinese characters hung on the walls. Heavy red satin curtains, always drawn across the windows overlooking the street below, gave the dining room a morgue-like ambience.

It was a hot, very sultry Tuesday afternoon in late August 1969. Steve and Jan Curry were arriving from England via cruise ship. Jan planned to study economics at the University of the West Indies, while Steve would work in the government's Central Planning Unit (CPU) as an economic planner. Gladstone Bonnick, CPU director, asked us to meet Steve and Jan and look after them during their first few weeks in Jamaica.

Within a few hours, like chameleons, their snow-white British skin turned flush pink to match the temperature. Steve's brow trickled with perspiration while Jan fanned herself with anything and everything handy. Tropical depressions floating through the Caribbean summer had deposited lots of water, so the mosquito troops abounded. Scouts looked constantly for "new blood." Steve and Jan, of course, fitted that profile. A canvas of red polk-a-dots soon appeared on Jan's exposed English legs. So, I suggested that we escape the heat and mosquitoes by having dinner at Jing Wah, whose most attractive feature in summer was the air conditioning.

At half past five, the restaurant was nearly empty. A waiter, wearing a well starched and impeccably pressed maroon jacket with black trousers showed us to a table towards the rear of the dining room. A gale of laughter from the only other party, a group of men seated behind us in a large booth, sailed past us and died in the belly of the red curtains across the room while we were studying the menu.

Suey Mein was the only thing I ever ordered from Jing Wah's Cantonese-Jamaican menu. Suey Mein, served in a large white porcelain bowl decorated with blue flying fish, consisted of a clear broth with floating rice noodles, miniature corns on the cob straight from a tin, water chestnuts, snow peas, green onions, thin ham strips, shrimp and Chinese pork dumplings. The suey mein arrived at the table steaming hot, the best way to consume it because the temperature inside Jing Wah was like a London fall day's temperature.

While Jan and Steve peruse the menu, I tune into the animated conversation at the table behind us. Five white Jamaican men babble in loud jocular voices. Soon one shouted roughly across the dining room to the waiter, "Come here na mon."

The waiter stopped first to take the orders from our table and then continued to the men. Jan sat quietly. I couldn't tell if she was feeling tired, culture shocked, or if she's just a reserved English girl. Meanwhile, I hear the group behind us ordering another round of Red Stripes and Appleton rum on the rocks.

Then a rough voice snarled at the waiter, "Bring dem drinks, now, mon. Get your black backside moving, na mon."

We all hear the voice. The conversation at our table ceases abruptly.

The voice continued to mutter Jamaican-isms like "rasclat, bumbaclat..." which I assume neither Steve nor Jan could understand. Without warning, anger struck me as the rough voice continued to hurl insults at the waiter who, by now, had slunk off to the far side of the dining room.

I turned around in my chair, throwing a dagger look at the men, saying curtly, "Please, treat the waiter with respect, so we can enjoy our dinner."

A tense hush came over them. We resume our conversation just as the waiter served us our order. Within moments, however, a small ball of rice sailed over my shoulder and lands on the black polished table in front of me. Following the rice bomb in rapid succession, a series of vegetable torpedoes hit our table. We turned just in time to witness the rough voiced man loading his soup spoon with another torpedo and then using it as a catapult to launch the food bomb in our direction.

Immediately, I snapped indignantly, "Stop that right now!"

The rough voiced man grabbed his fork and knife, jumping to his feet and lurching forward towards our table, looking prepared to assault me with his cutlery.

Robert stood up and so did the other men at the rough voiced man's table.

"Leave my wife alone. Sit yourself down and behave yourself," Robert shouted vehemently.

The other men surround the rough voiced man, clucking, "Com'on na mon, sit, down, calm yourself, na mon, have another drink," steering him back toward the booth. Then they sandwiched him between themselves inside the booth.

I could barely keep myself from laughing. That is, until I looked across our table at Jan and Steve. The flush pink color has disappeared; they both appeared pale and very English again. I am thinking that Jan might just dive under the table any second with Steve following her. My heart palpitated noticeably. My knee jerk reaction to defend the waiter's dignity had upset the entire evening. Robert shook his head disapprovingly in my direction.

Saturday afternoon, we went to eat lunch at Thora and Georgie's home. Recounting the Jing Wah incident had everyone in stitches over the rice bombs and attempted cutlery assault.

Thora asked a lot of questions about the rough voiced man.

"What did he look like?"

"Short, swarthy, unshaven beard—probably the only other white man in Jamaica besides Robert with a beard."

"Oh, a beard! That must be Mickey Hadaad, Moshe's son. He's crazy to ras, mon!" she exclaimed. "They keep him down in Ochi because he so troublesome."

We laughed a lot over Mickey's food catapult and the terrified looks on Steve and Jan's faces. And, we went back to Jing Wah as soon as possible to eat more suey mein.

~

Even in November 1969, after one year in Jamaica, every day serves up fresh experiences. So much energy leaps out from the rich musical sounds to be heard everywhere: on the streets, radio, in rum bars and even hotel clubs. Ska, calypso from Trinidad, drumming from Africa and the newest of the new – reggae music – is being born. I am learning to dance West Indian style at parties or on the rare occasions when we go to the Courtleigh Manor Hotel in New Kingston with friends to enjoy a live band.

Publications like *The Third World Quarterly*, a journal published by young intellectuals at the University of the West Indies, *Abeng!*, a radical newspaper for popular distribution, and revised histories like *Capitalism and Slavery* introduce me to post-colonial perspectives on the English speaking West Indies. Popular Caribbean writers are exploring their African roots; roots I'd never thought about before living in Jamaica. Playwrights, actors, and dancers look away from Britain towards Africa for creative inspiration.

Meanwhile, my job has been a straight up disappointment. The director of the educational planning unit in the Ministry of Education has yet to assign a single task for me to complete. When I ask him for direction, he promises something for tomorrow or the next day but never shows up to fulfill the promise. Each day at the Ministry becomes an exercise in figuring out what to do with the time between 8:30 am and 4:30 pm.

The library beside the educational planning unit has become my unofficial office. It's a small square room lined with bookshelves. What makes it really pleasant is the eastern view from an expanse of plate glass windows which look upward towards the magnificent Blue Mountains standing like a group of ancient elders robed in dark green to protect the plain of Kingston-St. Andrew. Filled with sample school textbooks and children's books, there is also an ample collection of sources on education and educational planning. Reading everything that's available becomes my way of puzzling through the basics of educational planning. This turns into part of my daily routine.

By now, I've visited a number of schools across the island. The visits are an eye opener. Many schools look like three sided barns constructed of wood with one side open to the air and roofed with zinc. All the classes are housed in undivided interior space with only standing chalkboards separating one class from the next. While the structure is not uncomfortably hot, the noise level drones at the din of a factory. The children sit two, three or sometimes four on a bench attached to scuffed wooden desks. The teachers stand at the front of the class and if lucky might have their own desk.

Some of the children are barefoot. All are wearing uniforms: girls in navy blue pinafores with white blouses and boys wearing khaki shorts and shirts. The uniform, to be purchased by the student's family, is a condition that must be met to attend school. Children without uniforms are not allowed to come to school. The teachers have a stern and authoritative countenance. The children recite poems, stand up when called upon and endure numerous ruler slaps across the knuckles when they give a wrong answer or aren't paying attention. I am shocked by this systematic use of corporal punishment. I have never been witness to this in any educational institution I attended during my entire eighteen years of formal schooling in California.

The physical conditions in some of the newly constructed schools are somewhat better. However, the educational atmosphere seems to be the same: children crowded into small desks, copying, reciting and getting slapped. When I discuss this with my colleagues and friends, no one seems the least bit surprised. The indifference, and therefore *de facto* acceptance of hitting students as an integral part of the endorsed pedagogy, deeply shocks me. Following these forays into the schools, I turn my attention to reading every government document about the country that I can get my hands on. Robert passes me things from his work at the Central Planning Agency where he is happy as a clam and busy as a worker bee. We are like day and night in our dispositions towards our work.

~

Ted introduced me to the sociology department at the UWI where I was offered a part time job as a tutor for a class of first year sociology students. This provided the challenge of along with the opportunity to use the library of the Institute for Social and Economic Studies. With so much to learn about Jamaica, present and past, as well as the Caribbean and the colonial history of the region I welcome the university work. The barrage of new ideas and information as well as novel experiences from every day life constitute a gigantic jigsaw puzzle that I am constantly trying to piece together. Maybe someday I will be able to draw them together into a bigger picture of this post-colonial Caribbean reality.

Because Jamaica has only been an independent nation for six years, heated debates prevail about the road to development the country should follow. The specter of the 1958 Cuba Revolution falls like a long shadow across the island.

Only ninety miles northwest, intellectuals at the UWI intensely debate the Cuba model of development versus the capitalist approach to de-colonization. Robert's family members seem to favor strong ties with England and the United States. Many West Indian intellectuals, however, are looking elsewhere for direction.

In fact, Walter Rodney, the Guyanese historian who was denied re-entry to Jamaica just before Robert and I arrived in October 1968 was banned for teaching about and advocating "Black Power". Jamaican economics professor George Beckford—commonly known as "G. Beck"—published *Persistent Poverty*, an indictment of neo-colonialism as a legacy of plantation societies like Jamaica.

Jamaica's bauxite industry is one of the new engines of the post-colonial economy. Foreign multinational companies like Alcan, Alcoa and Reynolds scrape the raw red bauxite rich earth from the tender tropical surface then ship it to the US, Canada and Norway for refining into aluminum. The foreign companies wholly own the bauxite industry. This generates a lot of controversy. "Shouldn't Jamaica get more in return for this valuable natural resource?" ask economists at the UWI.

At the same time, with Cuba cut off from the Western hemisphere by the United States' economic and political blockade, Jamaica is trying to promote itself as a major Caribbean tourist destination. Hence the travel poster that grabbed our attention in London luring us to the island. But, within the Jamaica Tourist Board, a debate rages. Should the country be marketed simply as a tropical paradise for foreigners, almost exclusively of European and North

American origin? Or should Jamaica try to sell itself as more? For this reason, a new series of travel posters are produced. These posters depict tropical fruits, the colorful higglers (Jamaican market women) and scenes from the interior of the island with a large caption reading

## JAMAICA: MORE THAN A BEACH

~

Elizabeth Ramesar introduced me to Richard Johansen who was developing an information system for the MOE. Placed in the Ministry by USAID (United States Agency for International Development), unlike other "experts," Richard was working on his doctorate at Harvard. He also distinguished himself from the others by marrying a Jamaican girl and manifesting interest in questions of the country's development path.

Richard and his wife lived in "Beverly Hills". Built recently, their house clung to the hillside and commanded a view of the lower Kingston-St. Andrew plain. Upon occasion we were invited to dinner and Richard, Robert and myself speculated about strategies for education and development in Jamaica. We weren't exactly in the position to implement these strategies. However, in the future, we could hope to be.

Regulars on the diving expeditions, I knew that Richard and Joanne liked water as well as the beach. Through Ronnie Manderson-Jones, we had discovered that the government owned some choice properties scattered across the island and that these could be rented by civil servants for less than five dollars Jamaican a night. During these years, the Jamaican dollar was pegged at rate equal to the US dollar making five dollars JA affordable for us. On several occasions we invited the Johansens to join us for a weekend.

One of the properties was a wood cottage at Duncans between St. Ann's Bay and Falmouth. Located on a beach hidden from the road by sugar cane fields, snorkeling at Duncans surpassed any other diving experience I had in Jamaica. The reef was growing less than fifty feet from the shoreline and it wasn't more than a quarter mile in length. Untouched by regular divers, shell creatures, tropical fish, eels, brain coral and branch corals abounded. The reef scratched the water's surface at low tide. When snorkeling at Duncan's, I felt like a gull gliding over the water, peering into the mysteries below.

~

Continuing to meet people I might not have met in a country much large than Jamaica, I found myself playing tennis at the Senior Common Room, the university's faculty club. As a tutor in the sociology department, I had access to the courts. Always a mediocre player, I admired the strength and skills of the West Indians who frequented the SCR. With the exception of Noel Chutkan, all the players who played at the SCR were male. Noel came regularly to play with her husband, a doctor at the university hospital. She had both tennis form and technique combined with strength and stamina. Noel was also a principal dancer in the National Dance

Company of Jamaica, which performed annually at the Little Theatre.

I admired her athleticism as well as her artistic talent as a dancer. Eventually we became acquainted and occasionally rallied. Once in a while Robert and I would catch a game of doubles with Noel and Winston. They politely indulged us.

At that time I harbored hopes of improving my tennis game. Then one evening when we were invited to dinner at the home of Jim Trowbridge, the Ford Foundation's Caribbean Representative, I discovered that his wife, Suzie, played weekly in a women's double game with Noel. Since the Trowbridges traveled often there was talk of my substituting Suzie when she was off the island. That never happened because I worked and didn't feel comfortable taking off time on a weekday to play tennis, even though I was rarely fully occupied at the Ministry.

Through work I began to rub shoulders with the fly by night representatives of the Inter-American Development Bank (IDB) who came to town from time to time. They worked with upper level Ministry personnel—not me—but also at the Central Planning Unit. I remember quite clearly attending meetings at the CPU as a Ministry of Education representative with two IDB-ers, both American, and intent on collecting demographic and financial data. About ten of us were corralled in a small room at the CPU that was poorly air conditioned and filled by an immense mahogany table. To enter and exit the room, one had to squeeze between the table and the walls. The only decoration on one wall was a photograph of Eddy Seaga, Minister of Finance at that time.

The meeting was dragging. Half past four had come and gone. Louise, the server/cleaner, continued to bring glasses of iced water. I was thinking about tennis followed by a swim at the university while the IDB-ers continued to talk data and money. When half past five slipped away and the light began fading, Louise locked the front and back entrances to the CPU as well as the door to the meeting room. Located between Jonestown and downtown Kingston, the CPU was a residence converted into an office building. Other houses in the area had been converted into "yards" as monied Jamaicans moved up the St. Andrew plain towards Red Hills, Stony Hill, Beverly Hills and the Blue Mountains, leaving the downtown neighborhoods to deteriorate into a series of densely occupied slums. The area wasn't particularly safe, even in the daytime. Locking us in was Louise's way of protecting us and the CPU from people on the street who might decide to walk in. This had already happened and the visitors were looking for more than a glass of water or an inside view of a government agency.

Louise lived in Trench Town, Seaga's district. She's was a JLP loyalist and unswerving Seaga supporter. Why shouldn't she be? She owed her job at the CPU to Seaga. Who else would employ an aged, semi-literate Jamaican woman?

The IDB team kept pressing us to organize more data, and make additional calculations which they deemed essential to complete their mission in Jamaica. I did not know at the time that they were hired consultants whose fees exceeded my annual salary depended on certain deliverables. They were intent on keeping us there until they got those deliverables. Others gathered round the mahogany table insisted on leaving, one by one. Ainsley had children to collect. Ann had a colleague waiting for a ride at another office. Dawn had a doctor's appointment she couldn't miss. Tony had a radio show to record. These personal commitments were met with resistance by the consultants. However, with politeness and determination, the Jamaicans, each and every one, managed to extricate themselves from the locked quarters.

By six thirty, only three were left with the two consultants: Robert, Steve and me. Just as we were wrapping up the calculations, one of the consultants said,

"Oh, wait a minute, we need to convert everything from Jamaican to US dollars."

"Come on," I protested feeling fed up with these pushy Americans. "You guys can do that when you get back to Washington." I walked to the locked door knocking insistently for Louise. When the door opened, Louise peered into the room looking from the consultants, to Steve and Robert, to Seaga's photograph and back to me trying to decide whether or not to let me out.

With the requisite diplomacy, Robert rose addressing the consultants, "Thank you, and we'll look forward to seeing you next time you're in Kingston.

~

Since arriving in Jamaica, an awareness of who I am, and who I am not, grows. Neither Jamaican nor expatriate; undeniably white of

European origin, however, wanting to reject what it means to be "white" in Jamaican society, I sometimes feel a prickly discomfort from  often mistaken for a Peace Corps volunteer rather than a young professional working at the Ministry of Education, who wants to be taken seriously which didn't seem to happen very much. After more than one year, I was taking stock of the situation.

Years later, when I worked for the World Bank, I heard an inside story about the "planning" job at the MOE.  UNESCO recommended that the Ministry of Education establish an educational planning unit to administer a promised loan from the World Bank.  For the Government of Jamaica to get the loan, the World Bank stipulated the establishment and staffing of an educational planning unit as a pre-condition. Thus the Jamaican government was under pressure to hire "planners" to fulfill the imposed condition.  My boss, Keith Taylor, had spent time in Paris at the International Institute for Educational Planning.   However, the two expatriates hired into the unit, Ted and myself, were more like paper place holders to satisfy World Bank conditions than real professionals expected to work on planning Jamaica's educational future.

Robert, however, had settled further and further into Jamaica life. He loved his work and felt highly valued. He was excited about exploring his long forgotten Jamaican roots. Like a fish back in water, he responded enthusiastically to the sociability of Jamaican society and to the feeling of being in the thick of making history in an emergent nation.

What were my options? My thoughts turned to possibility of further training as an educational planner. This kind of training could be had in Paris at UNESCO headquarters. Then I considered the information provided by Richard Johansen about doctoral programs at Harvard, University of Chicago and Stanford. The next step was to write to each requesting information. After investigating a bit more, I decided to apply to all three programs. I encouraged Robert to do the same. However, he was uninterested. So I decided to file applications on his behalf as well as my own. To this initiative, he made no objection.

In January, a recruiter from the Stanford program passed through Jamaica and arranged to meet with me. Over a drink at the Terra Nova hotel, one of Kingston's most exclusive hotels, he queried my application to Stanford's SIDEC (Stanford International Development Education Center) with skepticism.

"Well, we currently have one female doctoral student. However, she already has one child and a baby. Her husband is a lawyer in San Jose. We don't expect that she will ever really work in the field of international education once she actually finishes her doctorate."

"That's a bit different than my situation," I countered, trying to refute his reasoning. "After all, I am living in Jamaica working in the field right now and my husband is an economic planner with the Jamaican government. I want to learn more so I can return to Jamaica and work in the field." He nodded with a look of disbelief.

Fast-forwarding to 1981, more than a decade later, I met Richard Johansen again. He hired me at that time as an educational specialist in the Latin American Educational Projects Division of the World Bank. Three years later, Marlaine Lockheed, the female doctoral candidate who wouldn't work in the field of international development education, was also hired by the Bank and worked there for nineteen years until she retired in 2004!

After this unpropitious visit, doubt clouded the possible success of my graduate school applications. So, I considered another option: starting a family. Robert's cousin, Annabel, who was exactly our age, already had one little girl and was expecting another.

"Motherhood, that's what life is about!" she exclaimed with such conviction. I hadn't thought much about motherhood. It seemed like such a distant possibility. But, now, with the unlikely chance of returning to graduate school, motherhood might be an option.

~

In early April replies from both Harvard and the University of Chicago arrived. Disappointingly, the results were negative. However, there was no word from Stanford. I waited another two weeks, and still no news from Stanford. Finally, I decided to try to make a telephone call. To my surprise, I actually reached the professor with whom I had been corresponding. When I asked what had happened with my application, he replied with a question:

"What has happened with your husband's application for doctoral studies at Stanford?"

His question came as a bit of a shock: Is my acceptance contingent upon his being accepted? While I didn't speak my thought, I certainly pondered it. When I reported the conversation to Robert who decided to make a visit to Jim Trowbridge at the Ford Foundation's Caribbean office. With speed and support, Jim contacted the people he knew at Stanford. Within a week, the application for doctoral studies had been confirmed! Moreover, the Foundation was offering Robert a fully funded four-year fellowship.

Jim called us over to deliver the good news. Then I asked for a bit of clarification: What about my application?

"Well, yes, you've been accepted, but we thought that you could do the Master's degree program at SIDEC."

"But I already have a Master's degree. I want to study at that the doctoral level," was my response.

Robert quickly spoke up on my behalf, and very convincingly. By the time the conversation was over, we were both going to Stanford in September to begin doctoral studies, fully funded by the Ford Foundation!

# THE GREEN TORTOISE
# (1970 - 1972)

*Dear Ariel and Zahava,*

*When least expected, life has a way of working out. Robert and I were both accepted to study for our doctorates at Stanford University. Once again we are to buy one- way tickets. This time the tickets take us from Kingston to San Francisco. Stanford, known as "The Farm", is where we will spend some of the next four years. The biggest surprise, however, is news from the ante-natal clinic at the University of the West Indies hospital: We are going to be three! Conceived in the Caribbean, your mother is to be born on The Farm, soon after we begin our studies.*

*Granny Sherry*

Chalyn held by Robert, Sherry, Stanford 1971

# HOW CHALYN
# GOT HER NAME

$O$uch! Stop, that doesn't feel very good," I tell the baby sticking its toes up under my ribs. "Come out soon, we're just about ready for you!"

The yet to be born baby motivates me to finish all the reading, writing and exams that need to be completed during my first term of doctoral studies. When I am not studying, I'm arranging the baby's room. By late October a small white wicker bassinet waits in the middle of the second bedroom at 116 A Escondido Village. Staring at the empty bassinette, with the baby still in my tight, fat tummy, I try to wrap my mind around who will be sleeping there in just a few weeks. I tingle with excitement and uncertainty.

Will the baby be a girl or a boy? We don't know. We do know, however, that we want a special name for our baby – a name that has a special meaning to us. Nineteen seventy is a year when new parents are giving their children "unusual" names. The hippies of our generation, also called Flower Children, anoint their babies with names like "Rainbow," "Magic," and "Stardust." Our Jamaican friends Horace and Jenny call their first child "Talawa," meaning strong, feisty and not to be underestimated in Jamaican patois. Lance, a Rastafarian, and his English wife, Louise, call their bi-racial daughter, "Zebbie," a nickname for Zebra.

Ultimately, Chalyn gets her name from all the new experience Jamaica has given to Robert and me. One evening, still in Jamaica, I read some poetry by Edward Braithwaite, a Bajan poet and professor of literature at the University of the West Indies. One poem speaks of the Kings from Saleen who lived long ago in West Africa. These kings are reputed to know where to find a fountain of light that gives life and spews happiness. "Saleen", the sound rolls in my mind even when the rest of the poem disappears. I tell Robert about the Kings of Saleen wondering if they could be the inspiration for the name of our baby to be born later that year?

In the months to come, "Saleen" echoes in my thoughts and I continue to play with the name, improvising around many possible sounds. Although we have left the island, its beautiful beaches, lush mountains, broad plains, and lumpy hills that Jamaicans call "the cockpit country" remain vividly present. I can still see the rich tangle of trees growing on the steep slopes of the Blue Mountains: mango, guango, star apple, and breadfruit, along with banana, cacao and coffee woven into a dark blue green quilt. Distance doesn't erase these special sights, smells, tastes, or stories of Jamaica. Reggae still beats heavily in my ears. And while I have, as yet, to make sense of all this fully, by now these sensations have become part of me.

Then on November 21, 1970, many thousands of miles from Jamaica, our baby is born in Redwood City, California: a beautiful tiny girl weighing just 5 pound 13 ounces. This is the baby who will sleep for the months to come in the white wicker bassinette that has been waiting for her at 116 A Escondido Village. Made in Jamaica and destined to return, we call her "Shalen Arica." "Shalen" for the Kings of Saleen and "Arica" for Africa.

The nurse brings a birth certificate form the morning after she is born. I write "Shalen Arica" on the certificate. When Robert comes to the hospital, I show him the birth certificate. Asserting fatherly prerogative, he takes the pen scratching out "Shalen" and changes the spelling to "Chalyn." And that's how Chalyn got her name—a fountain of light and wellspring of happiness.

~

A few hours after Chalyn arrives, the nurse brings her to me asking, "How are you going to feed the baby?"

"What do you mean?" I ask, while thinking to myself, "What a funny question."

"Are you going to nurse the baby or give her a bottle?" the nurse inquires.

"Oh, I don't know. I haven't really thought about that before. I guess I'll try to breastfeed her."

Wrapped tight in a white blanket with a silly pink ribbon taped to her head, already covered with dark brown hair, the nurse puts baby Chalyn into my arms. I cradle her next to me while she nuzzles up to my breast and begins sucking.

"This is a good start," I tell myself. Her sucking gives a little relief to my ever so taut breasts that look and feel like they are full of silicon.

Once at home, overloaded with free baby bottles and infant feeding formula samples, I quickly discovered that breastfeeding the baby is  much easier than using a bottle; the milk's always there, warm and ready, no bottles to wash or sterilize. I also learn that mother's milk is nature's quintessential fast food and am surprised that no one has ever mentioned this to me.

The first night Chalyn comes home, Robert decides to make a special dinner. He seasons a Cornish game hen with thyme, rosemary and garlic and roasts the hen in the oven with lots of yummy potatoes. Lightly steaming some fresh green beans while preparing a delicate garden salad decorated with cherry tomatoes, he then carefully sets the dining room table. Two candles stand in the center of the table, a romantic touch to   celebrate the homecoming of our new princess.

While Robert makes dinner, I am upstairs trying to put Chalyn to sleep. First I feed her seated in the rocking chair. The clock says 6 p.m. when she starts nursing. When she stops, the clock says, 6:47 p.m.

I lift her as gently as possible and place her tummy down in the center of the expectant bassinette. She looks so peaceful and delicate lying there. Covering her with a small yellow crocheted baby blanket, I zip up my lime green and pink quilted bathrobe ready to tiptoe out of the room in pursuit of the warm gamey smells gliding upstairs from the kitchen. Just as I reach the bottom of the stairs, a cry squeaks from her room.

Quickly, like any well-intentioned new mother, I shuffle back up stairs and peek into the room. The crying grows louder. Chalyn's face begins to turn pinkish red. I tiptoe over to the bassinette and pat her back gently. Then the crying increases.

Robert comes upstairs and stands in the doorway looking quizzically at us. "Maybe she's hungry," he suggests.

"I just finished feeding her," is my tentative reply.

"Maybe she needs burping," he says. Robert actually knows more about babies than I do. He had two younger brothers and a younger sister, growing up. Sometimes he helped his mother with the babies, especially, his youngest brother who came along when Robert was already sixteen.

So Robert picks up Chalyn and holds her next to his shoulder and starts patting her gently on her little back. After a while, she makes a sound so tiny that it seems like a mini-hiccup. After Chalyn burps, he puts her back into the bassinette. She lies there quietly, and we both turn to sneak as softly as possible downstairs to our waiting feast.

The table looks so inviting with the lighted candles. Robert brings the food, surrounding us with hot tempting fragrances. We sit down and pick up the wine glasses. Just as we lift the glasses, sparkling with flecks of candlelight, to our thirsty lips, I hear some noise coming down the stairs. Could it be?

"Listen," I say to Robert. "Do you hear anything?"

We sit in silence momentarily, and yes, a noise reaches us, and it's getting louder by the second. I gaze at the warm lovely dinner waiting in front of us. The hands of the clock are pointing to the seven and three, it's 7:15.

"Let me just go upstairs and check on her," the words habor both of concern and ambivalence.

By the time I reach Chalyn's room, the cries are loud and strong. No problem with this baby's lungs, I muse. But she can't be hungry, can she? I just finished feeding her. Next hypothesis: maybe she has a poopy diaper? Picking her up quiets the crying a bit. Then I try the diaper hypothesis. Voila, a splash of bright yellow-orange newborn poop. Reaching for a clean cloth diaper, I call to Robert, "Could you please bring me a warm damp wash cloth?"

Fifteen minutes later, bottom washed, a freshly pinned diaper covered with plastic pants, I pick up baby Chalyn. Instantly she starts nuzzling my chest like a hungry piglet.

"It looks like she's hungry," I comment to Robert, who looks on for moral support. "I'll just sit down in the rocker and feed her a bit more to see if she'll go back to sleep."

So we begin another round of nursing which lasts until about 8:15. When I put Chalyn down into the bassinette again, she immediately begins to cry. Robert comes back upstairs to do the burping routine. Meanwhile, the candle light dinner has cooled on the table.

She cries and stops, cries and stops. I nurse her, put her down, nurse her, and put her down. And, of course, she cries. A bit after 9:30, I put her down again in the patiently waiting bassinette and, it's almost unbelievable—she stays very quiet.

"I think she's exhausted. I am! Let's try to eat dinner and go to bed!"

The next day, I call the pediatrician to ask about a baby that keeps crying and nursing and crying and nursing.

"Oh, many little babies do that at night. Their stomachs are so tiny that they can't get very much milk in at any one time. She's just tanking up again and again so she can get a good sleep. The tanking up will stop once she's bigger and can hold more in her tummy."

Chalyn continues to tank up every night for the next six weeks. This puts an end to candlelight dinners for quite a while. By early January, her tiny tummy seems big enough to hold the milk she needs to sleep from eleven at night until six o'clock the next morning.

~

Nearly six weeks were wedged between Chalyn's birth and the beginning of the winter quarter of graduate studies. I needed every minute of this time to begin learning how to be a mother. Robert talked with our Cuban-American next door neighbors who told him that women shouldn't go outside the house for two weeks after giving birth! That was a long time for me to stay cooped up inside, but it also gave me time to rest, relax and get adjusted to Chalyn's presence in my life.

It didn't take long to fall absolutely in love this perfect new being. Everything about her was lovely: her bright blue eyes, her tiny hands and feet, her beautifully shaped round head. Even her disposition was dialed to agreeable. She didn't cry unless she was hungry, tired or in need of a diaper change. What good fortune to have all my time with her the first weeks of her life.

Being a graduate student and young mother simultaneously proved to be challenging, but far less isolating than work at the Ministry of Education. Within the first week at Stanford, I met two others in the SIDEC program: Marlaine and Jean . Both would quickly come to be important sources of support while at Stanford as well as long time friends and colleagues.

Marlaine, already in her third year of study, was the very person who the Stanford recruiter had described as being "unlikely to work in the field of international development education". Outgoing, intense, at times outspoken on her own behalf—a trait considered to be especially unfeminine at the time—she reached out to me immediately.

I had arrived at Stanford seven and a half months pregnant without any fore mention of this fact. Marlaine already had shaggy, blond headed Graham, then five, and Khalida, not quite a year old. Khalida had penetrating crystal blue eyes that lit up her delicate face. Her name was Afghani because Marlaine had served there in the Peace Corps. At Stanford, she had helped to open the door for women who wanted to combine studying for an advanced degree with motherhood despite the skepticism of certain faculty members. More than a decade later, Marlaine would join me at the World Bank to prove the inauspicious predictions of the recruiter—who shall remain nameless—wrong.

Jean was a first year doctoral candidate as was I. The second daughter of a large Irish Catholic family, Jean already had an adorable two year old, Heather, with gentle milk chocolate eyes that admired her mother. Jean and I bonded in our second term when we jointly produced a simulation game, Neurland, designed to illustrate the cooperative survival strategies used by the Neur, a nomadic herding tribe in East Africa. Thus when Chalyn arrived, she was girl child number three to be born to a SIDEC doctoral student/mother.

By early January 1971, when classes began again, I had already decided that I didn't want to leave Chalyn with a babysitter. She was so precious that I wanted to keep her close to me all the time. This meant that Robert and I instituted a regime of switching off baby-sitting. When I had a class he would watch Chalyn and when he had classes she stayed with me. There was, however, one seminar that we attended together. That's when I decided to take Chalyn to the university with me. Normally I carried her around in the snuggly on my chest. This wouldn't work for going to class. I needed something that she could sleep in for an extended time. The solution was to buy a used stroller. The stroller we purchased was painted lime green with a matching fringed canopy top, made in China. We paid only five dollars to some neighbors in Escondido Village and christened it the "The Green Tortoise."

Chalyn strolled to campus on Thursday afternoons in the Green Tortoise. During the stroll, she would inevitably fall asleep by the time we reached the seminar. I would walk into the room quietly and push the stroller under the seminar table where she could sleep unobserved.

The seminar participants hailed from around the world: Brazil, Peru, the Philippines, Venezuela, Mexico, Colombia, and countries in Europe as well as North America. They were surprised, but delighted to see a baby coming to class. The professor politely accepted Chalyn's presence quite possibly because she napped for most of the afternoon. He didn't seem to mind having a sleeping student in the class. Moreover, because SIDEC was still a young program, the most of the professors were young themselves and in the midst of raising families. This, I believe, made them empathetic to the juggle between the academy and family life. The atmosphere for the women graduate students was, on the whole, supportive.

During the spring term an imposing, stocky German professor in his early thirties, conducted the seminar. His recipe for the subject, education and politics, was quite tasteless and dry. Instead of sitting down and stimulating discussion he stood stiff and ponderous at the front of the room. Sometimes he lectured without stop for most of the three hours. His English was accurate but heavily accented, posing a challenge for those whose native language wasn't English. Full of theory, a heavy cloud of formality hung over the seminar proceedings. Students didn't say much. Meanwhile, Chalyn slept quietly in the Green Tortoise.

A warm, June day near the end of term, the professor took a risk. He decided to tell a joke, the first joke of the term. Eyes around the seminar table were soft and drooping. Still talking his way through the third hour, he suddenly stopped speaking then looked out at us. A mischievous expression spread across his face. I hadn't seen this look before. His large body relaxed just before he began to speak. "Vell, in Europe, you know..." and he was off rambling through a joke towards a distant punch line. Reaching it, he paused appropriately, and a few seconds of silence floated across the room.

Suddenly an unexpected wail came from under the seminar table. Chalyn woke from her long nap in the Green Tortoise stealing the punch line. The seminar exploded into laughter. Poor professor, his mouth dropped open, wide enough to catch a fly. His face went flush pink. He stood in front of us, speechless.

This was my opportunity to make a quick get away. Grabbing the Green Tortoise while motioning apologies, I quickly pushed Chalyn out of the seminar. Her university days had clearly come to a close, and she was barely seven months old. These first seven months of her life and our first year of graduate school had been intense, but thankfully, both Robert and I were young, healthy, and energetic. And I felt especially grateful to be at Stanford studying about education and development, a dream I wasn't sure would ever come true.

Life in Escondido Village was ideal for married couples with young children. Having so much to manage with a new baby and both parents studying, the simple convenience of our daily life in the Village made the challenges possible. I know now that all new parents should have access to such a flexible, supportive way of living. Located on the Stanford campus just minutes by foot or bicycle from the heart of the university, our apartment was simple, comfortable and easy to take care of. Living in the midst of other young parents made cooperation around the details of daily life feasible. Shopping by bicycle at the Palo Alto Co-op meant that we rarely needed to use a car. And, the Stanford campus was superbly endowed with every facility imaginable including swimming pools, sports fields, tennis courts, squash courts, a golf course and even several public schools.

From left to right: Chalyn in Gerry Pack, Robert with
Robbie and Joe Douthwaite over looking the
Caribbean from the hills of Portland, Jamaica, 1971

# GERRY PACK BABY

We rented a Gerry Pack from the Escondido Village children's supply deposit to carry baby Chalyn on our backs. In fact, most baby and toddler gear we needed came from the deposit overflowing with every imaginable baby and toddler item. Five dollars for a Gerry Pack; fifteen dollars for a crib, three dollars for a changing table-- incredible luck, because our graduate stipend from the Ford Foundation only totaled $500 a month for the three of us.

Chalyn, now seven months old, sat on the hammock-like seat of the Gerry Pack, stubby legs sticking out beneath the ocean blue canvas that is stitched to an aluminum frame carried on the shoulders of one of her parents. If she wanted an even better view, she could just push her little feet against the bottom of the frame, stand up, then peek over her porter's head like a little princess carried on a palanquin.

The Gerry Pack quickly became an indispensable travel aid during the summer of June 1971. Robert was anxious to get back to his job at the Central Planning Unit in Kingston. So we packed up 116A Escondido Village leaving Stanford in June for Jamaica. I am really looking forward to having time to be just a mother for a few months, even in the tropical summer heat of Kingston. Therefore, I make no commitments either to myself or any one else other than spending time with Chalyn. To prepare for the trip, I stuffed a couple of suitcases with clothes then wrapped up a large cardboard box of disposable diapers which have become indispensable.

Chalyn rode regally in the Gerry Pack through the airports between northern California and Kingston. When we arrive, the hot Jamaican summer rolls over us like a delightfully relaxing massage. My first intention is to introduce Chalyn to the best tropical luxuries: mangoes and swimming in the warm waters of the Caribbean. Robert's parents, Helen and Billie have always raved about the water at Doctor's Cave in Montego Bay. Chalyn gets her first dip when we arrive in Montego Bay from Miami. We have arranged to stay for one night in a local hotel near the beach. Immediately after dropping the luggage in our room, we head for Doctor's Cave where Chalyn bobs contentedly in the sea with a bright red water wing on each arm. The water was every bit as transparently blue, calm and swimmable we had expected it would be.

"Maybe this is the way motherhood should be?" I muse, "Lots of time to play with the baby without the pressure of studies."

Our stay in Kingston began with Thora and George at Paddington Terrace. My first concern about baby Chalyn was to protect her from being eaten alive by mosquitoes. Mindful of the Jamaican saying, "Mosquitoes love fresh blood." I sprayed her with repellant and made sure she slept under a mosquito net. Within hours of application of the mosquito repellant, my eyes and lips swoll up, itching like crazy. Nevertheless, it took time to figure out that I was allergic to the repellant. Fortunately, Chalyn wasn't. With hyper vigilance, she stayed bite free and the itchy swellies eventually deserted me.

Chalyn reaches for her first mango at Paddington Terrace, 1971

After Thora and Georgie's, we spend the next few weeks in the house of an Australian couple who has returned to Sydney for the summer. The house is located near Kings House in a small development scheme. I get my first taste of being a stay-at-home mom. I don't really like it in this suburban setting. There's no place to walk to with the baby; no one to talk to and the summer heat is fierce. Some friends tell us that we can move into the house they share with another couple at the base of the Blue Mountains. I am enthusiastic about making a change. It will be cooler there and more company for both Chalyn and me.

The mountain house, a rambling wood country-style place, has a large dining room, four bedrooms, and a big sitting room. The house dwells in an unkempt garden of miscellaneous guava, mango and mahoe trees that mix among tall feathery bamboo stands. The call of birds awakens us in the morning; the buzz of cicadas sings to us in the afternoon and the crickets and bullfrogs serenade us at night. Wild and matted against the hillside, the garden didn't offer much outside play space, so Chalyn spent a lot of time on her hands and knees polishing the hardwood floors inside while perfecting her crawling skills.

We shared the house with an Irish couple, John, a UWI student of tropical medicine, and Valerie, a nurse. Having developed a taste for hot pepper-like foods while living in Jamaica, they insisted on making curry at least three or four nights a week. John concocted his unique peppery mixture of spices into a curry paste. That's when curry revealed itself to be a changeable potpourri of spices like turmeric, cardamom, ginger, and peppers rather than a ground premix tin that I might buy in the market.

On weekends we often travelled to the country. One weekend we drive to Port Antonio to visit Richard and Mary Douthwaite. Richard had joined Robert and Steve at the Central Planning Unit in 1969 to conduct a study of the contribution of tourism to the Jamaican economy. Tall, outgoing, with disheveled hair, Richard was passionately interested in appropriate technology. He and Mary had lived on a houseboat while he studied economics at the University of Essex. Rather than live in Kingston, Richard, Mary and their two young boys moved to a small house in the hills above Gordon Town. Without electricity, they used kerosene lanterns for light at night; acquired a baby donkey as a pet for the children and gardened with dedication.

By summer of 1971, the Douthwaites had moved to Portland, at the far northeastern tip of the island. Richard had become involved in a project to build ferro-concrete hull fishing boats. The project intended to improve the fishing capacity of the traditional Jamaican fishermen who used small wooden launches with outboard motors which severely limited their fishing range. Also, the launches could hold only a small catch due to their size and lack of refrigeration capacity. Richard convinced the Jamaican Government to give some financial backing to the project along with several private investors.

Again, the Douthwaite family chose to live off grid. They had acquired land in the hills above Port Antonio with a sweeping view of the coast. Mary, a energetic strawberry blonde with her fair share of freckles, was home schooling the boys and putting energy into being a country mother. At the same time, she had become friendly with a neighbor who had a brood of nine children while expecting another. When we arrived late Friday night to introduce Chalyn to the Douthwaite family, they had a chubby Jamaican baby girl to introduce to us. Apparently, Mary and the neighbor had agreed that the Douthwaites could adopt the ninth baby shortly after she was born. The past eight months had been spent making arrangements to make the adoption legal. To Mary's chagrin, when she and Richard went to Kingston for the court hearing to finalize the adoption, the presiding judge had rejected their application. The judge thought it was inappropriate for a white, English family to adopt a black Jamaican child. The fact that both the biological and the adoptive parents had mutually agreed was not figured into the decision.

This reminded me of the heart wrenching visits which Robert and I had made to an orphanage in Kingston during 1969. The babies and toddlers were in small cribs, one after another lined up in a large room. A little boy, not more than fourteen months old, stood in his crib, insistently smiling for attention. When Robert picked him up, the child didn't want to be put down again, so great was his thirst for affection. With few attendants, the babies received little more than food and diaper changes. I had left the orphanage feeling despondent. How could someone bring a child into the world and then abandon it? And how could someone else deny a baby the possibility of a caring home and family?

~

During that summer we were able to manage a trip through Jamaica's Cockpit country. The lumpy mountains rose and fell, clothed in a vegetative weave of numerous green hues. Winding and twisting down the north side of this extraordinary terrain formed by porous limestone, we chanced upon a small village hanging on the hillside. Robert got out of the car to take a few pictures of this remote yet picturesque setting. Across the road a man was walking towards us. As Robert clicked several photos, the villager shouted and came running towards us brandishing a machete. He was taking great offense at being photographed, demanding that Robert give him some money for taking his picture.

Amused, but not cowed, Robert laughed while telling him, "If you don't want to be in my picture, move out of the way."

This provoked an extended exchange between the two, and resolved itself when Robert asked for the man's address, offering to send him a copy of the photograph. After a bit more altercation, an agreement was reached. Robert would send Mr. F.O. Curry a copy of the photo. Mr. Curry explained that his initials, FO, stood for Mr. "Half a Fool" Curry.

Several months later, Robert received an effusive letter, quoting passages from the Bible as thanks for the photos he had sent. This was a good reminder that Jamaicans were sensitive about being treated as objects of curiosity by apparent tourists as well as appreciative when appropriately acknowledged.

~

The Gerry Pack really justified itself on our return trip to California. We stopped in Mexico City to visit Elena, our friend from graduate studies in England. When we arrived, I put Chalyn in the Gerry Pack to carry her off the plane. After showing our passports, the officer asked for proof of vaccinations. I handed him two small yellow booklets, titled "International Certificate of Vaccination," and written below in English and French, "as approved by the World Health Organization."

Examining the booklets, the immigration officer motioned to a short man with thick black hair, a broad forehead and small dark eyes. Wearing a white lab coat he began scrutinizing our vaccination booklets very carefully. After checking both Robert and my booklets he looked again at Chalyn's booklet and shook his head. "The baby doesn't have a smallpox vaccination," he pronounced in a careful singsong Mexican Spanish.

"No, she doesn't. Children under two years of age shouldn't have smallpox vaccinations. There's a danger that they could have an adverse reaction."

"She needs to have a smallpox vaccination to enter Mexico because she is coming from Jamaica," he replies matter-of-factly.

"There's no smallpox in Jamaica," I protest.

"She can't come into Mexico without a smallpox vaccination," he insisted.

A stubborn feeling swept me like a cold wind. I didn't want Chalyn to be vaccinated, fearful that she might have a fever or an uncomfortable reaction. So I dug into non-compliance mode continuing to argue with the health officer.

Meanwhile, Robert looked around anxiously for Elena who stood waiting and watching just on the other side of the customs area. He motioned to her for help. Somehow she managed to get past the customs' officials  arriving to mediate. After arguing with the health official to no avail, she whispered to me in English, "Just let them give her the vaccination and as soon as you're out of customs we'll go into the bathroom and wash it off."

"Brilliant!" I thought, "the Latin solution." And that is just what I did.

During the following week, we took a trip from Mexico City to the famous silver mining town of Taxco. My mother had spoken of this traditional hill town and even purchased an extraordinary ring—a purple amethyst set in a delicately sculpted silver grape vine—there. I wanted to see the place which crafts such beautiful jewelry.

The heart of Taxco, like almost every Mexican town, is a small plaza shaded by trees, dotted with benches, and accented by an old corrugated iron gazebo for the occasional band performance. Jewelry shops and restaurants ring the plaza while the rest of town spread out up and down the hillside. We spent a few hours exploring and then chose a small family restaurant for lunch. The young, dark haired waitress, enamored by Chalyn's bright blue eyes, whisked her away into the kitchen to meet the rest of the family.

After lunch we made a final stroll through the plaza.  An enormous silver and red striped tourist bus pulled up beside us and tourists pour into the plaza. They were Japanese tourists sporting cameras sporting enormous zoom and telephoto lenses. The cameras hung ready around their necks. Suddenly, several tourists took note of us walking by and within seconds, to my astonishment, I was in the middle of a circle of cameras. The shutters clicked furiously as the Japanese photographed the blond mother carrying her blue-eyed baby in a canvas pack on her back—a Mexican scene of extraordinary interest!

Sherry and Chalyn, Stanford, 1972

# FARM LIFE

$B$ack in 116A Escondido Village, following our summer in Jamaica, the reality of the coming year of study looms ahead. Taking Chalyn to classes is no longer feasible. She's too active and inquisitive. Certainly she won't sleep for three hours in the Green Tortoise anymore. Besides, I want to concentrate fully in class when I'm there and have no desire to be ducking out early. Already friendly and sociable, I think Chalyn would enjoy the company of some other young children. But, I don't want to put her in childcare for six to eight hours everyday. What I really want is a warm, loving family situation close to 116A.

Fortunately, Robert spots a notice for babysitting posted in the laundry mat near our townhouse.

He calls as soon as he comes home and arranges to meet Eve the next morning. Eve lives just a five-minute bicycle ride away in another part of Escondido Village. Eve's front door is open, so the three of us peer through the screen into a townhouse that looks very much like our own with a short hallway leading from the front door into a living room/dining area. Beyond are big sliding glass doors looking out onto to the back porch area with the large grassy courtyard beyond. On the patio a scooter, tricycle, wagon, small boy's bike and a big wheel sit in a jumble. And then we hear the sound of lots of footsteps coming down the stairs.

A young woman with fine brown hair pulled back in a bun, carrying a small very brown skinned child with giant dark eyes and thick, wavy black hair, steps into the hallway and greets us with a happy smile.

"Hi, I'm Eve, and this is Eden," she introduces herself and the baby as she pushes open the screen door inviting us in. Behind her are two young boys. One looks about seven years old and the other, smaller and more wiry, looks like he could be four or five.

"This is Vincent," Eve says, pointing to the older boy. "And that's Gregory," she motions to the smaller boy.

The children crowd around us with a friendly curiosity. Chalyn looks very interested in the new group of inquisitive faces.

"This is Chalyn," we say. "She's 10 months old."

"Is she walking?" Eve asks.

"Not yet," we reply.

"Eden is already one, her birthday was in July, and she races around after Vincent and Gregory everywhere."

Inside, we see that toys are strewn everywhere: blocks, balls, games, dolls, trucks and books. We put Chalyn down on the floor so she can crawl around to explore. Eden stays close to her mother, while we chat. We all immediately feel very comfortable with each other.

Eve is a full time mother and her husband, Kiki, is studying at the Stanford Business School. She comes from Michigan, describing her family as Jewish, and tells us that Kiki's family is Mexican, which seems to explain the children whose complexions and eyes are much darker than her own. Eve needs to make extra money and wants to do some babysitting at home. Vincent and Gregory will be going back to school shortly, and she thinks that it would be nice for Eden to have another baby in the house to play with.

We decide to try babysitting at Eve's house for a week. We don't plan to take Chalyn to play at Eden's everyday. She'll go there mainly on the days and at the times we have classes. This is how babysitting at Eve's begins.

Immediately, Chalyn and Eden become good friends and playmates. Although Eden could already walk, and in just a few months Chalyn was also toddling around with her. Their fondness for each other is apparent from the smiles they greet each other with every morning and the enthusiasm with which they play together. Sometimes, when we come to pick up Chalyn, she wants to stay longer to play with her friend Eden.

We integrate ourselves into each other's lives. Eve is part of a cheese-buying group. She invites us to join and share a wheel of jack cheese as big as a tricycle wheel along with several other families. I find a gymnastics class for toddlers not too far from Stanford and take Chalyn and Eden to classes there once each week. Then we find swimming classes and enroll both girls. That way, Eden and Chalyn can to learn together.

Eve babysits for Chalyn from September 1971 until December 1972. When it comes times for us to return to Jamaica for field research. We feel sad to leave Eden, Eve, Gregory, and Vincent.

By the time we return nine months later, baby Bion, Eden's new brother has been born. Eve now has her hands full with the three children plus a new baby so she isn't able to baby-sit for Chalyn anymore. That's when we find Sojourner Truth Children's Center where Chalyn will attend nursery school during 1973/74 while we are writing our dissertations.

When we leave Stanford in July 1974, we don't see Eden and Eve for many years. However, we manage to keep in touch with the occasional letter. Many years later, when we move to Washington D.C., Eden is living in Newton, Massachusetts, not far from Boston. We arrange a reunion for the girls. In the summer of 1983, when Chalyn is twelve and Eden has already turned thirteen, Eden comes to visit us for a few weeks. She is already quite a teenager and the two get along famously just as before.

Chalyn  (l) and Eden (r) playing with clay, 1973

# REVOLT ON THE FARM

The eighteen months spent on the farm between September 1971 and December 1973 overflowed with activity, not all of it strictly "academic". Stanford is frequently referred to as "the farm" because the campus was been built on 8180 acres of land. In fact, because there's so much land surrounding the campus, it actually does have the feel of a large, secluded farm. The land was granted to Leland Stanford, railroad baron in the middle 19th century by the United States government. Eventually, Governor and Mrs. Stanford decided to establish a university there in memory to their late son who died from typhoid at sixteen years of age.

During the early 1970s, the Stanford campus brimmed with political debate like most university campuses. Heated contention was generated over US involvement in the Vietnam War; many young intellectuals wanted to style themselves as revolutionaries; the Civil Rights and women's movements also fomented plenty of controversy. The tensions arising from Cold War politics in Europe and the anti- and postcolonial movements in Latin America and Africa also found their way into campus discourse.

Two economics professors at Stanford, Jack Gurley and Don Harris, organized a political economy seminar that drew graduate students and faculty from across the entire campus. Through the political economy seminar and the Women's Union founded by feminist students on the Stanford campus, I met other women graduate students outside my own program.

Because the women's movement was just getting underway a coherent analysis of women's situation in contemporary society was missing from the seminar. Together with several of the female members of the political economy seminar who voiced concerns about the invisibility of gender issues in the seminar's readings and discussions, I decided to help form a women's political economy study group. The group incorporated six graduate students: Amy Bruce (anthropology), Susan Carter (economics), Helen Chauncey (history), Laurie Hemboldt (history), Barbara Waterman (psychology), and me (education). Our meetings continued for several years while we were researching and writing our dissertations. Intellectual support groups like these made life academic life at Stanford dynamic and engaging.

Another study group, the *Kapitalist State*, focused on the hypothesized crisis of "late" capitalism, is formed by Jim O'Connor, then economics professor, then at San Jose State

University.   Both Robert and I decided to get involved. The group met monthly at 116A Escondido Village during the 1971/1972 academic year. Through this group I got to know Kay Trimberger who would become a life long friend and colleague. Several of our Brazilian colleagues also joined the study group, introducing the concerns of dependent economies like Brazil's into the mix of ideas being discussed.

The tenor of these times stretched beyond the world of ideas to experiments with new life styles. A group of young faculty members decided to purchase an enormous brown-shingled house together, which becomes widely known as "The Embarcadero House." (Duncan and Helene Foley, Bridget O'Laughlin, Shelly and Renato Rosaldo, Jens Christensen—a graduate student in economics). They too experimented with organizing a communal life style.  A steady stream of parties, dinners and informal get-togethers flow through the Embarcadero House which quickly became a center for young, progressive Stanford faculty and graduate students.   The Embarcadero House was just one of a number of collective living groups in the area,  others integrating students and community members.

We become engageded in our own little experiment in cooperative living: together with three other couples we form a dinner cooperative.   The dinner co-op was Isaura Belloni's brainchild.  Isaura, a Brazilian, was one of my classmates in the SIDEC program.  We met the first day of our first SIDEC seminar at Stanford in September 1970. At that time Isaura could hardly speak English. With huge, penetrating blue eyes she didn't fit my stereotype of a

Brazilian. This picture came from Anna Maria, a Brazilian graduate student I knew at the University of Essex: Anna was tall with dark hair and eyes and frequently laughing or joking.

By contrast, Isaura was fair-haired with a very determined and serious demeanor. When Robert and I shopped for the first time at the Palo Alto Co-op market, we spotted Isaura with her husband who had a lion's head of strawberry blond hair. I whispered to Robert, "She must be married to an American." Of course it turned out that I was completely mistaken. Benicio, her partner was as Brazilian as Isaura. They both hailed from the far south of Brazil, Rio Grande do Sul, where there had been a lot of immigration from Italy and Germany in the early part of the twentieth century. Benicio's family was German and Isaura's from northern Italy.

When Isaura appeared at 116A Escondido Village the day after we returned from the summer stay in Jamaica , she came with a proposition:

"Sherry, why don't we form a dinner co-op during the week so we don't have to spend so much time cooking?" I immediately liked Isaura's proposal. It made so much sense, so that's exactly what we did.

Isaura already had the people in mind: Robert and I, she and Benicio, Bill Flores and his wife, as well as another couple who were friends of Bill. The dinner co-op would function Monday through Thursday evenings. One night at each couple's home.

The first attempt at the dinner co-op, however, flopped. Benicio and Isaura lived in a one-bedroom apartment on the 6th floor of Blackwelder high-rise apartment building immediately next to our townhouse in Escondido Village. We could walk to each other's places in two minutes. Bill Flores, however, lived a twenty-minute drive from the Stanford campus in Mountain View. Moreover, both Robert and Benicio liked to cook while Bill and his friend followed a more traditional pattern: the wives did the cooking and cleaning up while the husbands did the eating and the socializing.

This first dinner co-op only lasted a few weeks. But Isaura persisted. A month later she recruited two other Brazilian couples: Evelina and Pedro along with Glaura and Malori, all of us PhD students, with the exception of Pedro and all living in Escondido Village.

Monday evenings we ate at 116A. The first night Robert prepared a Jamaican curried chicken while I cleaned up the mess. On Tuesday night Benicio made a beef stew and Isaura did the washing up. And so it went. The dinner began at 6:30 and finished promptly at 7:30 so we all could move on to studying. If it was my turn to cook and I had a meeting or something else to do, I would leave the meal ready and waiting for the others.

Via the dinner co-op, we developed strong academic and friendship ties with our Brazilian colleagues. Robert, Benicio, Evelina and Malori collaborated on the first edited volume of essays published in English on dependency theory, *Structures of Dependency*, under the guidance of Frank Bonilla, a professor of political science. Dependency theory was a critique of neo-colonial relationships that had evolved between Latin American and economically power nations of Europe and North America following Latin American independence movements of the nineteenth century.

This critique was generated mainly by Latin American social scientists. Frank Bonilla arranged for Fernando Henrique Cardoso, the Brazilian sociologist noted for his work on dependency theory, to spend a term at Stanford working with the dependency study group. Decades later in 1995, Cardoso was elected president of Brazil ushering a new period of democracy and economic growth for that nation.

Being incorporated into this little "Brazilian mafia" changed the quality of our social life at Stanford. These friends loved Chalyn who was just learning to walk when the dinner coop began. They taught her a few words of Portuguese and offered to babysit from time to time. Moreover, the Brazilians were party animals. They loved to organize *churascos* (barbeques) on the weekends and instituted a volleyball game every Tuesday late afternoon. We were lucky to always be included.

Isaura also introduced me to Paulo Freire, the great Brazilian educator whose ideas about a community-based approach to adult literacy spoke to me. I found Freire's perspective intriguing and relevant because I had worked as a volunteer literacy instructor in Jamaica.

Involvement with the Brazilians peers often felt more natural than with the American radicals at and around the Stanford campus. Several professors from the Stanford campus (Bruce Franklin and Juan Flores) spearheaded a political group known as "Venceremos" (We Will Win). This group took the Leninist ideas of "armed struggle" seriously—or as seriously as middle class American intellectuals seemed to be able to take them. Several women graduate students from the political economy seminar belonged to Venceremos. All this was part of the ethos of the times. There was so much experimentation everywhere even in the highly privileged, monastery-like ambience of Stanford.

However, I had neither the time nor the inclination for something that radical. Martin Carnoy's seminar on education and the economics of development provided the    both technical tools and critical analysis for understanding for some of the circumstances that I had observed in Jamaica. I viewed these ideas as potentially helpful when I would return. In the sociology of education course I took with Professor Elizabeth Cohen, the theory of status disability she used to study the ways in which interactions in classrooms function to transmit/reproduce pre-existing inequalities among students fascinated me. I could see the applicability of these ideas to the punitive teacher/student interactions I had witnessed in Jamaican schoolrooms.

Everything wasn't entirely smooth sailing. In a seminar on modernization with Alex Inkles, he and I disagreed vehemently. I remained insistently radical in my critique of his theory of modernization and he was equally intransigent when it came to tolerating different viewpoints. It was a classical example of two individuals sticking to their guns not wanting to look for common ground. Instead we locked in an intellectual tussle focused on who was going to win the debate rather than how could we reach understanding. The disagreement became so intense that Inkles decided to trade me for another doctoral student, Alejandro Toledo from Peru, without discussing this matter with me directly. When this happened I was relieved not to have to work with him on my dissertation.

For a dissertation, the study of the impact on the Jamaican and Cuban models of development on women was my first choice. However, I couldn't find courses or faculty at Stanford to facilitate this work. An international and comparative gender focused topic had no currency at Stanford, at this time. Ultimately, I was not able to muster the kind of support that I needed to do research in this area. By the end of the 1971/72 academic year, I re-focused my topic to a study of teacher-pupil relations in Jamaican primary schools. In this way, I could test the theory of status disability in the Jamaican context and work with Professor Cohen.

# CHILLY IN CHILE
# (1973)

*Dear Ariel and Zahava,*

*In January 1973, we leave "The Farm" for Jamaica again. We have several small suitcases and five large boxes of chocolates. Our plan is to conduct field research in Jamaica for our dissertations. However, instead of round trip tickets from San Francisco to Kingston, we again have one-way tickets. We have been selected to attend a two month seminar at the Latin America Faculty of Social Sciences in Santiago, Chile. The seminar brings together scholars from the Americas to examine and discuss what's happening in "socialist" Chile exactly at this time.*

*Granny Sherry*

# A BOX OF CHOCOLATES

Each time we returned to Jamaica from California our suitcases were loaded with one-pound boxes of See's Candies. A treasured sweetness from southern California, we brought the chocolates as presents for Ruby and Stanton, Thora and Georgie, the Aunties on Trafalgar Road and several of our friends including Marlene and Ronnie.

By January 1973, Ronnie and Marlene had moved to a lovely apartment in Stony Hill with a commanding view the Kingston-St. Andrew plain. They invited us to stay with them until we got settled in a place of our own. Happy to be away from winter, we decided to put pleasure before the business of getting settled again in Jamaica for the coming six months of research. A small cottage in Negril belonging to WISCO (the West Indies Sugar Company in Westmoreland) was available for rent.

At this time, Negril was still an untouched paradise. The only sign of people was one large old colonial house at the seaside surrounded with rock pools where three large sea turtles lived. Just beyond, the two WISCO cottages sat on the hillside viewing the quiet spaciousness that stretched southwest along the pristine seven-mile beach. Somewhere far up the beach was a lone hotel, "The Sundowner". However, rocky cliffs above deep pools of transparent blue water at the eastern end of Negril were preferable for swimming and diving to the flat beach shallows.

When heavy rains hit Negril, the black shelled land crabs' underground burrows flood. The crabs needed to look for higher, drier shelter. It was easy to find them at night along the ghostly-unused stretch of highway flanking the beach. When the car headlights shone on the crabs, they would freeze. The tire iron came in handy for catching these creatures, because the crabs would inevitably grab of the iron hold with their big claw. Dangling from the tire iron, it could be placed into a burlap crocus bag. After a few days, a strong rain came in the late afternoon. When night dropped over the sea, we headed out for the hunt. Within forty-five minutes the crocus bag was full. We headed back to the cottage to cook the crabs with scotch bonnet peppers for seasoning. We then ate them along with chunks of hard dough bread. Yummy!

After five days of relaxation in Negril, we felt ready to return to Kingston to get on with the dissertation research mission. As soon as we arrived in town, there was an invitation from the Aunties for one of their delicious Jamaican lunches of fricasseed chicken, Johnnycakes, rice n' peas, fried plantain, and bread pudding for dessert.

One box of See's chocolates was a gift for the Aunties. They insisted that these were the absolute best chocolates one could eat. Just as we were readying ourselves to walk out the door of Ronnie and Marlene's flat, I remembered the chocolates stored in the freezer before our trip to Negril.

Mmie was a totally organized housekeeper. She refused to have a "helper" even though she worked full time at the university. Amazingly, she prepared a week's worth of meals on Sunday, storing each one in the freezer. That way there was no cooking to do when she arrived home from work. So far as I could detect, her views hadn't been affected by the women's movement as had mine. She was intellectually as bright as Ronnie minus the volatility, acting as a calming influence over frequently turbulent waters. She amazed me by cooking meals for every weekday on Sunday then storing them in the freezer.

Quickly, I checked the freezer compartment stuffed with frozen casserole dishes, rummaging around to locate the chocolates. How difficult could it be to find five boxes of chocolates in the normal size refrigerator's freezer left there just six days before? However, I couldn't find the chocolates, so I begin to doubt my memory.

"Robert, didn't I put the chocolates in the freezer before we went to Negril?" I queried in a puzzled tone of voice.

"I don't remember," he called to me from the hallway.

"Could you check in the big suitcase to see if I left them there by chance, please?"

I continued to search the freezer, taking each item out and placing it on the counter. Still I was unable to retrieve any chocolates from the recesses of the freezer.

"Nope, there aren't any chocolates in the suitcase," he shouted back to me.

"I can't believe it. I'm sure that I put them here before we left for Negril!"

The search for chocolates intensified. No chocolates were to be found, not in the freezer, the refrigerator, nor any of our suitcases.

"Let's get going or we'll be really late to lunch," Robert urged.

~

Lunch at the aunties had been a tradition since we moved to Jamaica in 1968. They invited us to both lunch and tea at Trafalgar Road just across from New Kingston, the uptown hotel and business area with its modern, high rise buildings sealed off from the tropical weather with large glass windows and air conditioning. The Trafalgar Road house has an ample tile veranda with a group of high backed white wicker rockers designed for comfort and extended visiting.

The aunties were three: Muriel, Doris and Freda, all Henriques. Mimi was the eldest: tall, thin, with fluffy white curly hair. She wore wire spectacles that slid down the narrow bridge of her nose. Years ago, in the 1920s, 30s and 40s, she ran a little school that many of relatives attended: Granny Ru,

Grandpa Billie, Auntie Do, and Granny Helen all went the school as small children learning to read, write, recite and do their numbers. Mimi was also well known in Kingston during the teens and the 1920s because she played the piano to accompany silent movies in the open-air theatre at Cross Roads.

The sisters live together like three spinsters although Mimi had been married to Alan, an English military man, who died in the Second World War. Dodo and Frieda never married. Nonetheless, Frieda had a suitor, Sweetie, a good-natured widower who often came to Trafalgar Road to sit on the front porch and visit. While visiting, of course, everyone sipped tea sweetened with condensed milk and occasionally played a friendly hand or two of bridge.

Gwendolyn was the fourth, honorary auntie. Small, slightly shriveled like a brown peanut shell, her smile seemed broader than her tiny face. She sparkled with laughter and good humor, flitting about the house like a firefly that lights up every canto. Gwenie came to work for the Henriques when she was just fourteen, almost the same age as the aunties at that time. Since then she had lived and worked with the aunties, first at Studley Lodge near Cross Roads across from the Nutall Hospital and now on Trafalgar Road attending to the three sisters every need.

When we come to the aunties for lunch, it is Gwenie who attentively serves us. We sit at the big round mahogany table set with silver, white linen napkins and a little silver bell that Mimi rings to get Gwendlyn's attention. From the first lunch we have with the aunties, Gwenie discovered that I love Johnnycakes – fried white flour biscuits – that Robert likes bread pudding and that we both are endlessly thirsty for the Trafalgar Road lemonade made from fresh fruit picked in the yard that the cook sweetens with brown sugar. So any meal we eat with the aunties will certainly include Johnnycakes, bread pudding and lemonade.

When the aunties, Mimi, Doris and Freda learn that Robert and I have come back to Jamaica for six months, they tell us about Mandala Cottage.

"It belongs to Martin and Shirley Aub, and I believe that they might rent it to you," says Mimi.

Both Martin and Shirley teach mathematics at the University of the West Indies. Irish Town is perched far above Kingston in the Blue Mountains. It's cool and quiet in Irish Town far away from the bustle of Kingston. The aunties tell us that Shirley and Martin have three young children who I imagine might be playmates with Chalyn.

After lunch Robert telephones to inquire about the cottage. Martin tells him that Mandala Cottage is vacant, and that we can rent it for $25 Jamaican dollars a month. Then he invites us to come up to Irish Town to inspect the cottage.

Late in the afternoon we returned to Ronnie and Marlene's place, excited by the possibility of finding a temporary home in the cool of the Blue Mountains. I also queried Marlene about the chocolates. A most uncharacteristic look of embarrassment spreads across her face.

"Oh, I thought that they were all for us," she replies in a tone of concocted innocence.

"So what happened to the five boxes, is the question?"

"Well, I ate them," Marlene looked thoroughly ashamed.

Disbelief struck me, and I began to laugh.

"You mean you ate five pounds of chocolates in five days? Wow that must be worthy of a place in the Guinness Book of World Records!"

# MANDALA COTTAGE

Nestled in the Blue Mountains, Irish Town was a community of subsistence farmers who for hundreds of years lived simply, growing enough food to feed their families. However, in the 1960s, a few "big people like Alexander Bustamante, the first prime minister of Jamaica/founder of the Jamaican Labour Party, and the Rolling Stones built luxury getaways around the Irish Town area. And, we soon discovered, a few other people like us (academics, artists, and writers) were living up there as well. Irish town refugees wanted to escape the heat of Kingston along with the constant talk of who's been robbed or assaulted and who's sleeping with whom whether this be friends, family or the politicians.

Mandala Cottage, named after Hindu art designs, came as a surprise. To reach the cottage one had to leave the Newcastle road and drive about a mile down a steep dirt track. A few small wooden and cement block houses popped up along the road side before it disappeared into a dead end at the Aub's rambling wooden country house with a faded red zinc roof. Set up on a flat knoll, the house boasted a three hundred and sixty degree view of the mountains. To the west, the Caribbean Sea spread like a bright, narrow turquoise ribbon on the horizon.

We parked the little Ford Escort just purchased from David Silvera. The Aubs, Martin and Shirley, emerged from the house flanked by their two boys: Nelson, six and Michael, five, while their little sister, not quite two, remained cloistered inside. They met us as we walked up the stone steps towards their veranda. Quickly diverting us down the across a grassy patch, they led us down another set of stone steps, descending to a patio in the shade of an enormous guango tree. The guango spread over our heads like an enormous green parasol with black pods dangling from the branches. The tree was perfectly proportioned, making a gigantic umbrella during daylight. The real surprise came later when we observed that its leaves folded up to sleep at night.

Mandala Cottage had an oversized door that opened in a friendly way onto the patio. It was a simple wooden cottage with a pitched roof. Inside the ceiling was an open network of planks and beams making the square room seem larger and more airy than it actually was. Sparsely furnished with only three chairs and a wooden table, I thought, this could due for the next few months. A closet sized kitchenette had been tacked onto the back of the cottage which also served as a conduit to a narrow sleeping room beyond. The sleeping room had a loft bed and the Aubs promised to put a cot along the wall where Chalyn could sleep. The bathroom was another closet with a jerry-maundered shower, sink and toilet. I imagined that Chalyn might bath in the large metal tub on the patio for the coming months. Mandala Cottage met our minimum living standards: water, electricity, plumbing, a place to cook and sleep with a roof overhead. Without asking too many questions or pondering the decision, we told the Aubs that we would take the cottage. We needed only to drive back to Kingston to pick up our suitcases.

Mandala Cottage turned out to be as charming as it was rustic. The charm came from being situated on the edge of a small community of Jamaican peasant farmers in a dense tropical mountain forest. Most of the Irish Town families had lived here for generations. We could walk about a mile along narrow footpath from Mandala Cottage to the Irish Town bar and shop to buy kisko pops, hard dough bread, and The Gleaner, Jamaica's only newspaper at the time. The path wound up, down and around little cottages then ducked through thick plumes of bamboo stands, past a bumpy pitch in the forest where the village men and boys played barefoot cricket.

Nighttime settled dark and heavy on Mandala Cottage. The crickets, cicadas and croaking lizards serenaded us from dusk until sunrise. Some nights, we sat on the patio under the giant guango tree entertained by the flashing emerald lights of the peenie wallies – the Jamaican fireflies chasing each other in the black sky. Across the enormous gap between our mountain and Mauvis Bank, the melodious voices of the pocomania worshippers rang out. Pocomania is a Jamaican spiritist religion practiced by descendents of African slaves. Their ceremonies take place at night with much singing and dancing. Some people say that pocomania is a type of voodoo.

Our closest neighbors (besides the Aubs) were the Arnolds, a family of tall elegant people with very dark skin. Their grandchildren Warren, ten; Charm, nine; Titi, two; Mark, also nine and Shirley, six, came to visit the day we moved into Mandala Cottage. Warren, already tall for his age, had a handsome, seriousness about him. The smile of his slightly younger sister, Charm, was more than equal her name. And Titi, two years old like Chalyn, chatted and danced constantly. Soon Chalyn had learned many Jamaicanisms from the children and was speaking patois with a Jamaican accent. The Arnold children became Chalyn's constant playmates from that first Sunday in January until the day we left for Chile in late May.

From left to right: Chalyn, Shirely, Titi, Warren,
Charm above Mandala Cottage, Irish Town, Jamaica
1973

Chalyn and Titi on the steps of Mandala Cottage,
1973

The children always remembered their "pleases" and "thank yous". They accompanied us like faithful puppies wherever we went on foot. They delighted in playing with our kitten, Bumbles, and joined Chalyn in painting with the tempera colors we'd brought from California. Mr. and Mrs. Arnold occasionally stopped by to visit. Velma, the six foot tall mother of Warren, Charm and Titi was also a usual visitor at Mandala Cottage.

The only sad face in our life at Mandala Cottage was Vernie, the young woman we employed to help us. She'd just had a baby and rarely smiled. Only seventeen, she left school at age twelve. Her job was mainly to take care of Chalyn when we weren't at home. That really tugged at my heart because I didn't want to leave Chalyn up there in Irish Town with Vernie. She wasn't mean, but she seemed so sad. Maybe it was because she had to leave her own baby when she's at Mandala Cottage? I never found out for sure. Perhaps she didn't even know herself. Vernie hardly replied even when I asked her questions. Chalyn would cry when Robert and I would get into the Escort to go down the hill to do field work. So I ended up taking her over to the Arnolds frequently where she had all the other children to play with and felt happy.

On weekends we would go for walks in the forest around Mandala Cottage. One Sunday afternoon all five of the Arnold children came along for a walk down the mountain track below our cottage. Soon we met Mr. Savage with several of his cows. The children amused each other by touching the "shame ladies" growing between clumps of grass. The Latin name for shame lades is *mimosa pudica*.

Shame ladies look like tiny ferns with fronds the size a child's little finger. When touched, the pinnae, those miniature individual leaflets that make up each frond, close together.

Following the walk, Chalyn fell asleep on her cot wearing green shorts and a white cotton blouse covered with a pattern of dainty yellow and green flowers. Several hours later she woke up crying something very usual. When I unbuttoned and removed her cotton blouse, I could see that her back was covered with little black spots.

"Look at this!" I exclaimed to Robert. We peered closely, discovering that the spots were actually minute black crabs.

"I think these are tics." I was almost shouting as I continued to examine the swarm of little black dots. Worry pounced on me. Even though I'd never seen a tic before, I had read about tics: that they bite your skin and then start sucking your blood. Worse yet, I'd heard that once the tic attaches itself to your skin the only way to get rid of it is to cut it out or burn it off.

Robert went rushing up to the Aub's house. This must have been the only time one of us actually reached their veranda. Kindly, Martin came down to Mandala Cottage to inspect Chalyn's back.

"They're grass lice," he pronounced without any ado.

"How do you get them off?" I asked feeling the worry in my stomach.

"They breathe through their skin, so you just take some kerosene or gasoline and keep rubbing it on them. When the kerosene gets into them, they let loose and you can just pick them off."

That's exactly what we did. By rubbing lots of kerosene on Chalyn's little back we eventually picked off all the tics. After that experience, we were very careful to check Chalyn and ourselves after every walk in the forest. Occasionally, we found a tic or two. But with the kerosene cure, we could clean off the tics. This was a good lesson to learn, and a small price to pay for living in such an enchanted place as Mandala Cottage.

# CHILLY IN CHILE

By mid-May 1973, my research in twelve primary schools scattered across Jamaica had been completed. The observations from visits were to form the core data for a doctoral dissertation focused on the ways teachers related to their students. Using something called "status theory" the research asked questions like: Do teachers really call on boys more than girls? Do they give more praise to children whose skin is lighter in color than those who are darker? And are they more inclined to direct negative feedback to children who are perceived to be lower status?

Now the time to switch to travel mode arrived again. On the last day of May we will to fly much farther south to Chile. There we will participate in a two-month seminar titled "Methodological Approaches in Inequality Systems"! Organized by two professors, a Chileno, Claudio Fleisfisch, a political scientist at FLACSO (Latin American Faculty for the Social Sciences), and Hayward Alker, a political scientist at the Massachusetts Institution of Technology, we will be two of twelve graduate students – six from the United States and six from Latin America—participating.

The seminar's pretentious title provided an opportunity to look more closely at the ongoing experiment in democratic socialism being led by Salvador Allende who was elected president of Chile in 1970. By contrast with Cuba's revolutionary model, Chile symbolized the possibility of an electoral approach to increasing social and economical democracy within the country. Like the other participants, we are eager to examine the government policies and programs designed to promote greater equality as possible models for other places in the Americas.

Leaving behind the warm, Caribbean weather, the idyllic simplicity of Mandala Cottage and saying good-bye to Titi, Charm, Warren, Shirley, Mark and Mr. & Mrs. Anderson aren't easy. Since we plan to be back in Jamaica the following year, once our dissertations are written and accepted, the departure feels more like a "we'll see you later" than a final "good bye".

Twenty four hours later, ensconced in the airplane circling over a large city, butted up against a giant Andes mountain range, the Santiago appears below. The city spills down the lower mountains across an enormous flat plain. I will always remember Santiago as a gray city. For the two months while we lived there, the sky seemed to be perpetually dull and sunless. Buildings seemed to be cast uniformly in gray – covered with soot and air pollution. When Chalyn would run her fingers along a wall, as two year olds are prone to do, the tips turned almost black like those of a little chimney sweep. Imposing, heavy edifices, wide streets filled with weary looking buses blasting smoky clouds, honking cars, taxis and trucks were an emphatic counterpoint to the wooded footpaths and bamboo stands that surrounded Mandala Cottage.

When we deplaned to walk across the tarmac towards the airport terminal, I instantly felt the Chilean winter douse us like an unexpected cold shower. My first thought was, "Wow, we are going to need to buy really warm clothes for ourselves." This initiates a perpetual search for warmth in the months to come.

Claudio and his dentist wife, Carmen Gloria, have generously invited us to spend these two months at their comfortable three-bedroom flat on a quiet *cul de sac* in a suburb of the city. I am so grateful to have a place to stay waiting for the three of us.

Welcoming us, Claudio shows us a small bedroom with a double bed for Robert and me. However, there's no place for Chalyn to sleep. She's just grown accustomed to sleeping on a small cot near our loft bed in Mandala Cottage. Where will she sleep now? Carmen Gloria, with long, flaming auburn hair and bright blue eyes, graciously offers two cushions from the living room couch as a temporary solution. Now there's another top priority on our shopping list: a bed for Chalyn.

Over an improvised lunch, Claudio fills us in on the situation in Chile. Everything is very tense.

Opponents of the government have organized demonstrations: angry middle class homemakers take to the streets banging on empty pots and pans to protest food shortages. Workers in factories occupy the enterprises shutting out the owners. There is discord in the Congress even though Allende's socialist party holds an elected majority coalition government.

The economic situation is very difficult. Inflation is rampant, the Chilean peso is about 110 to $1 US on the black market, but pegged at 1 to 1 officially by the government. Claudio says there's a concerted effort to de-stabilize the Allende government by internal and external forces. The United States, one of Chile's main trading partners for copper, seems to be organizing an unofficial economic blockade. Sectors opposing Allende: the military, the wealthy owners of factories, large farms along with international companies have joined with the Nixon administration in Washington, D.C. to squeeze the government as hard as possible.

Claudio explains that the US Embassy is viewed by Allende supporters as the center of sedition being staffed mainly by CIA agents posing as the diplomatic corps. He lets us know in no uncertain terms that Americans in Chile are viewed with suspicion. He also informs us that Allende supporters have vowed not to use the black market to exchange foreign currency (mainly dollars) for Chilean pesos.

"El mercado negro es la estrategia principal de de-establizacion del goberno socialista de Allende." (The black market is the principal strategy for destabilizing Allende's socialist government.) We get his message, loud and clear:

"Don't use the black market to exchange your money, because if you do, you will be contributing to the down fall of the Allende government."

With this briefing in mind, we head out of the apartment to look for some warm clothes and Chalyn's bed. We need to get organized quickly. Today is Friday, and the seminar starts promptly at 8:30 am on Monday morning. Carmen Gloria directs us to a shopping area not far from the apartment. There are several boutiques with children's clothes. The prices, however, are fabulously high: one hundred pesos for a coat; sixty pesos for a sweater; fifty for long pants. Looking for a kid's bed is more discouraging. There doesn't seem to be anyplace to purchase a small mattress to put on the floor beside our bed.

Finally, after hours of searching, I insist on buying a navy blue wool sweater with narrow green and white strips woven across the chest. It looks like a little boy's sweater, but it's only 20 pesos, and I am sure that it will help keep Chalyn warm against the penetrating cold. Then there's a knitted *altiplano* Indian hat with earflaps to keep her head warm and a pair of long brown trousers. No frilly girl stuff unfortunately. I can see that Chalyn is going to need to be a brave little girl to weather the coming two months.

We eventually find a heavy gray overcoat for Robert, but nothing for me. By the end of the afternoon we have spent nearly half of our money on just a few items. How could ordinary, working Chilenos survive with prices like these? Thus the two-month ordeal begins. Claudio does everything possible to make our time in Chile comfortable. Since

163

I can't find an affordable winter coat he lends me his long, brown alpaca poncho. Carmen Diana has gone out of her way to locate a children's center not far from their apartment where Chalyn can stay during the day while we participate in the seminar. The center is in an old house recently converted into a nursery school for the children of professionals who support the Allende government. They tell me that Allende's grandchildren attend this center.

Leaving Chalyn at the day nursery each morning immediately becomes a dreaded routine for me. I feel both lucky and guilty leaving her at the childcare center. Guilty because she's had to make another big change in her short two and a half year life. This time to a place where she doesn't speak the language, Spanish, or know anyone. Chalyn, however, doesn't make a fuss. And within a few days, I feel more comfortable because the teachers are warm, kind and caring towards Chalyn as the little *gringa* newcomer. They have given her a *delantal*, sky blue smock/apron that all the children wear to keep their clothes clean while playing at the center. At the end of each day she has some creative project to show us: a finger painting, drawings, or a clay doll. She adapts to the Spanish language environment quickly. I feel grateful to know that she is safe and well cared for.

Meanwhile in the seminar we examine policies and programs which countries like Chile can adopt to reduce the unequal access to resources and wealth are scrutinized intensely. In 1973, Chile has about nine million people. While it is not the poorest nation in the Americas, many Chileans live without adequate housing, food, health care, and education, especially farmers and indigenous peoples (the Mapuches). Due to the long history of copper mining in the northern reaches of the country, trade unions are strong, confrontational about workers' rights, and believe in distributing a fairer share of the nation's pie among the poorest segments of the population.

None of these ideas can be taken for granted. A political and ideological firestorm burns intensely throughout the country. Polarized between staunch supporters of private property, foreign investment and economic privilege for the wealthy and militant advocates of a revolution which will be born from armed struggle, Salvador Allende tries to steer a middle course towards greater equality. But he seems to be caught between a rock and a hard place. Those advocating each of these two points of view don't really want to compromise or listen to the other's perspective.

In this mix of bitter disagreement, the United States has strong economic interests to protect: access to and investments in Chilean copper. Moreover, cold war politics are at play as well. The government of American president Richard Nixon, who will be forced to resign rather than be impeached, fears that the Soviet Union will gain a foothold in South America, like it did in Castro's Cuba. So not only is the weather in Chile chilly, but Cold War winds from the north sweep across the country.

When we're not at the seminar, we visit factories taken over by workers. Graffiti announcing slogans like "Workers' Power" and " The people united will not be defeated" are plainly visible everywhere painted on walls along with counter slogans. Thus the signs of confrontation abound side-by-side accentuating the grind of daily life in the cold of winter at the foot of the Andes.

I am particularly interested in learning more about improvements in social services like education and health. My rudimentary Spanish and being an "American" limits my access and understanding. However, I decide to focus on the government's efforts to expand child-care for working families – a service close to my own heart.

Children's centers have been opened in working class neighborhoods. It's easy to observe that a genuine effort is being made to provide clean, heated facilities with a supplemental food program for the children. The quality appears to be similar to what Chalyn has in the converted house she attends daily in a middle class Santiago neighborhood.

Sometimes, discussions at the seminar especially with the American co-leader, Alker, who tends toward abstraction and obfuscation, are frustrating. The most interesting moments are lectures by guest speakers from other parts of Latin America and Europe who have come to Chile like most of the seminar participants as sympathetic and curious observers. In particular, presentations by noted Brazilian sociologists living in exile, Theotonio dos Santos and Fernando Henrique Cardoso (who we already know from his stay at Stanford in the spring of 1972) enliven the discussions even when the ambience in Chile feels so gloomy.

Occasionally, in frustration, I leave the seminar early to pick up Chalyn. However, the winter weather combined with a lack of inviting places in Santiago to spend time with a two-year-old limit our options. This problem, trying to stay warm, intensifies on the weekends. Robert, Chalyn and I begin to feel a bit "homeless". There's a saying, "after three days fish and guests begin to smell". Despite Carmen Gloria and Claudio's genuine hospitality, Robert and I sense that we are a bit like the smelly fish. It's hard to keep a two year old quiet and inactive for much of the day. And the rapidlyly deteriorating economic and political situation seems to be seriously affecting our hosts' spirits. We make every effort to get out of the apartment as much as possible to give them some privacy.

However, limited funds and the winter with make traveling within Chile unattractive and difficult. Finally, we discover a large park on the mountainside near the downtown. There is a train that ascends the slope and some not terribly well maintained swings, a slide and a few rusty climbing structures where Chalyn can scramble about.

To help out Carmen and Claudio we buy as much food and wine as possible. There's a bottle shortage in Santiago, which renders purchasing wine a small challenge. One has to bring the exact bottle to purchase a new bottle of wine. It's the ultimate act of recycling. When Carmen and Claudio decide to host a party for their anniversary we help them collect empty champagne bottles from friends going to various homes across the city to pick up the empties before taking them to the bodega for a filled replacement.

We adapt as best we can to the situation. Amazingly, Hayward Alker, the American seminar co-sponsor has brought a three-month supply of peanut butter and jelly with him from the US because he doesn't like Chilean food! While, I always tried to live by the motto, "When in Rome do as the Romans," and wouldn't dream of bringing my own food supply, I found myself longing for home in California.

Perhaps the most challenging aspect of being in Chile was being an American. It was akin to being white in Jamaica. At this moment, Americans are the emblematic enemy for many Chilenos. I feel apologetic about the United States government's foreign policy with its interventionist practices in Latin America, the Caribbean and southeast Asia and, consequently, empathize with the Chilenos. However, not all Chilenos see me as I know myself to be. I feel a bit like an involuntary character in the political novel, *The Ugly American* (1958). Making every effort to be as diplomatic as possible and keeping as much distance as possible from the perpetually distressing information about the United States government efforts to de-stabilize the political situation in Chile was a constant challenge.

Just two weeks after our arrival in Santiago, Robert and I left the apartment to drop Chalyn at the children's center on our way to FLASCO. The avenue, usually crowded with noisy buses, rusted trucks and small cars is almost empty. Half way down the block, Claudio comes rushing in our direction.

"There's a coup attempt underway," he announces breathlessly. "Go back to the apartment and tune into to the radio." Making an about face, we head back to the apartment and turn on the radio. Within an hour it has been announced that an attempted coup has been repelled. Citizens are being called to demonstrate their support for the Allende government.

Demonstrations have never attracted me. I don't like large crowds of people whether for protest, celebration or entertainment. From previous experiences with anti-Vietnam war demonstrations in the US and Britain, my stomach starts churning and my neck muscles begin knotting just at the mere thought of a demonstration. I know that demonstrations can easily turn violent. When one is submerged in a huge mass of people, menaced by police, army and even mere hecklers, getting away from a violent eruption isn't easy.

Salvador Allende addressing supporters,
June 1973

With a young child, I am even more reluctant to take any chances. However, I do want to see what is happening. When Robert, Chalyn and I reach the main road leading from the Andes into Santiago, a massive procession of people, trucks, and buses is funneling from the outskirts of Santiago into the city's center. I am moved and impressed by the rapidity and strength of the response to the attempted coup d'état. Hundreds of thousands of people stream down the broad avenue. I decide to stay with Chalyn at the edge of the crowd. Together we watch the human flow, which seems endless. I am elated by this evidence of the government's popularity. Nonetheless, I count the days remaining in Santiago wishing that closure to this experience were closer at hand.

When the time of departure arrived more than a month later, a feeling of relief swept over me at the prospect of returning to California. On the morning of departure, a taxi arrived in early morning darkness. The farewell to Claudio and Carmen Gloria was quick and without regret. The streets seemed eerie, almost too quiet, under a blanket of gray skies. Our flight to Mexico City is scheduled to depart at 9 am. Leaving the apartment at 6:00 am should provide plenty of time. However, we haven't anticipated the roadblocks being set up along the highways leading in and out of the city. Bonfires tended by men in heavy jackets flame across the road. At that moment we have become witnesses to the beginning of a trucker's strike that will eventually paralyze Santiago's transportation system and is an integral element of the plan to bring the down fall of the Allende government. Our driver reports that he will have to take some detours. We dart away from the highway through a warren of small streets lined by shabby houses. The trip takes an extra forty-five minutes to reach the airport.

The airport is already heavily guarded by armed soldiers. We rush to the LanChile counter to check in and dispose of our luggage. I have remembered to stuff a backpack of toys for Chalyn's amusement on the long flight north. At the immigration check station to exit the country, the official begins to ask many questions: Why have you been in Chile? Where and with whom were you staying? How much money did you bring to Chile? Where was the money exchanged? Fear begins to well up in my chest. When are the questions going to stop so we can get on the plane and leave this zone of danger?

Fortunately, traveling with a child eventually dispelled the cloud of suspicious questions. Turning on her two year old charm, Chalyn eventually disarmed the officer's brusque, intimidating manner. She smiled, spoke a little Spanish, showed him her stuffed rabbit, and his young, hard face began to soften. Finally, he shrugged his epauletted shoulders, stamped our passports and waved us out towards the damp tarmac. We were free to climb the metal gangway to the plane, which would carry us north to summer and safety in California.

# AT THE FINISH LINE
# (1973 - 1974)

*Dear Ariel and Zahava,*

*On the first of September 1973, we are able to move into a new townhouse in Escondido Village. I feel like I am home again. My work for the coming academic year will be to write a dissertation, and I am eager to get started.*

*Settling in to a routine involved getting my office set up and finding childcare again for Chalyn. On September 11, 1973 Robert calls me from his office on campus.*

*"There's been another coup d'etat attempt in Chile," he reported. "This time, however, it seems like it's been successful. Salvador Allende is dead; people are being rounded up and put in the national sports' stadium."*

*Before the 1973 military coup is over, thousands of people lose their lives, thousands more are imprisoned, some brutally tortured; many more flee the country before the government seals the borders and still others mob the embassies seeking political asylum. Claudio and Carmen Gloria are among those refugees who fled. Eventually, rumors reach California that they have gone to Argentina.*

*Historians now see the foiled coup that we experienced in June as a test run for the actual coup on*

*September 11, 1973. Extremely sad about what has happened in Chile, I am nevertheless thankful to be safe in California. A Chile solidarity movement coalesces quickly in the San Francisco Bay area and Robert and I join the efforts to provide support and asylum for refugees as well as mount protests against the United States' role in the coup d'état. This is how we met many friends we still know today including Eric Leenson, one of the founders of La Pena Cultural Center which is where you two girls have performed Chilean music with Los Mapaches.*

*Granny Sherry*

# A CRACKED SKULL

It's September first, and we're moving to a new townhouse in Escondido Village, 137 F. The kitchen is empty. We needed everything: salt, pepper, oil, bread, butter, spices, fruit, vegetables, cheese, cereal, dish soap, in other words, the whole nine yards. Hot and filled with summer, Chalyn and I head for the Palo Alto Co-op to buy groceries, both of us wearing shorts and tank tops.

Chalyn likes grocery shopping. I put her in the cart, cruise the aisles while she helps me pick out the things we need. Of course, she asks repeatedly for stuff that I don't want to buy. Junk food like "carrots in the bag" which is what she calls cheetos, those neon orange puffs shaped like worms, sealed in shiny plastic.

Because this is a really big shopping trip, we go to the store by car instead of on the bicycle. When we don't have lots to buy we would ride bikes with

Chalyn wearing her little white helmet seated behind me while Robert carried the groceries in the baskets on his bicycle. Today, however, we've purchased so much at the Co-op that the trunk and even the backseat of the Chevy II overflows with groceries.

In my hurry to go to the store, I have neglected to put the car seat in the backseat of the Chevy II. These are the "old days" when car seats for children were optional rather than being required by law. Nonetheless, it's only a few minutes drive from Escondido Village to the Co-op through the calm Stanford campus. On the trip to the Coop, Chalyn rode in the back, but on the return home she is sitting in the front passenger seat.

Mindful that Chalyn is in front, I drive slowly and carefully. Just two blocks from our place in the Village, I come to a gentle stop at the intersection of Serra and Olmstead on the southwest side of the Stanford campus. Despite my efforts at caution, Chalyn loses her balance, rolls off the front seat headfirst and lands under the dashboard with a thud. She immediately starts to wail while crawling up from the floor into my lap.

Blood gushes from the back of her head. Cradling her in my lap, her face to my chest, I drive slowly and deliberately to the student health center, just one block away. I can feel my heart thumping wildly. Carrying her with blood stained hands into the health center, the receptionist takes one big look at us saying, "Sorry we can't help you, because she's not a student. We only treat students."

"Yes, but this is an emergency and I am a student."

A nurse appeared. Together with the receptionist, they shoot me synchronized callous looks insisting, "No, we only treat students, you'll have to take her to the Stanford Medical Center."

Fury chokes me. I want to immediately grab them and shake some sense into them. However, all I can do is retreat, driving as quickly as possible to the Medical Center with Chalyn sitting in my lap.

Blood covered, I walked into the emergency room packed with suffering people. And then the bureaucracy begins. The need to register, show proof of identity and insurance, as well as give an accounting of what had happened. Inevitably, I am directed to sit down and wait. Finally, someone announced "Shay-lynn? Girling." No one ever seems to be able to pronounce my daughter's name correctly.

Shown to an examining room, the doctor, is a young woman wearing a starched white lab coat. Finally, Chalyn has stopped crying. The doctor looks at me then looks at Chalyn, then asks for an explanation. Following my explanation, she asks me to please step out of the room so she can examine Chalyn and stitch up her head.

"Why do you want me to leave?" was my incredulous reply.

"I wouldn't want you to faint while I stitch up the wound," she responded.

"If I were going to faint, I would have fainted already," I reply. She looked so young and inexperienced; even younger than I was at twenty-eight.

I could see a furrow of displeasure cross her forehead, but she didn't counter my refusal. I held Chalyn in my lap while the doctor began to examine the blood-matted hair on the back of her head. Pulling away the hair carefully, she marked off the wound shaving a clean patch around it, then injected some painkiller into Chalyn's scalp, and threaded a needle before making a few black stitches across the cut. Chalyn sat quietly, cooperating the entire time the doctor worked on her head.

Stitching completed, the doctor ordered me to take Chalyn upstairs into the hospital to have her head X-rayed.

"Why?" I queried.

"To make sure that her skull isn't cracked," she stated matter-of-factly.

Still covered in blood, we are led through the labyrinth of elevators and corridors to the X-ray unit, where a technician explains the head X-ray procedure. Chalyn must sit on a chair resting her chin on a shelf, while holding her head very still so the technician can take pictures of her skull.

Chalyn tried very hard to cooperate. Nevertheless, she is still less than three years old, just a little girl—a little girl who has just had a bloody head cut stitched up. Three times the technician tried to get clear pictures. Each time, the X-ray blurred slightly because Chalyn couldn't hold her head completely still.

"Well, I think we will just have to put her down on the X-ray table and take the pictures there."

"What do you mean?" An alarm began ringing inside me.

"We'll strap her to the X-ray table so she won't move and then take the pictures."

"Strap her to the X-ray table?" That sounded very much like cruel and unnecessary treatment. A loud voice shouted inside me, "No! No! No!"

Facing the technician full on, I told her "Nope, we're not going to do that. I am taking her home right now."

"You can't do that," the technician asserted. "We need to X-ray her head."

"No, she's going home with us right now," Robert, who had joined us by now, insisted while scooping Chalyn up into his arms.

The technician called a nurse; the nurse called a doctor. They thronged us demanding that Chalyn have her head X-rayed.

"Not now, we're leaving." That said, we walked out of the Medical Center heading for Escondido Village.

Naturally, a cloud of doubt followed us. Had we really done the right thing by leaving without having a clear X-ray of Chalyn's head?

Once we are in our townhouse and feeling more secure, Robert decided to call a doctor friend about the X-ray. The friend's opinion confirms our action.

"Howie says that we did the right thing. Even if Chalyn's skull had been cracked the treatment would be the same: just stitch up the wound. Obviously, they wouldn't put her head in a cast. Howie thinks that the only reason they ordered an X-ray is to protect the hospital. He says that we should keep Chalyn awake for some hours to make sure that there's no concussion."

Chalyn recovered quickly. The next morning she was up and happy to be back playing around in

Escondido Village. But I have learned a very important lesson about avoiding cracked skulls: never take a small child in an automobile without a car seat just like the rule: don't ride your bicycle without a helmet!

# A PLACE TO WRITE

The clock of our Ford Foundation fellowships continues to tick. There are only ten remaining months to write my dissertation before the fellowship will expire. Quiet covers the Stanford campus those first few weeks in September before the term is about to begin. It's the perfect time to begin work on the dissertation. The first step is to get my office in the School of Education organized. To my surprise I have been assigned a new office mate, a fellow graduate student from Peru, named Alejandro Toledo. I heard through the grapevine that Alex was away at this moment. Thus I anticipated having the space to myself for at least three weeks.

Loading the baskets of my redwood brown Raleigh bike with books and field notes, I made the first foray to Cubberly Hall where my office was located. Collecting the key, I lugged all the materials downstairs through a warren of hallways in search of the office. The cool and dimly lit basement erased the tempting heat of summer helping me to feel more ready to get down to work. I placed everything on the cement floor in front of the office then unlocked the door. Peering into utter darkness I reached with my hand to scan the wall for a light switch. My fingers found the switch and with a simple flick dull white fluorescent light spread across the tiny room revealing two desks, each facing a different wall. I knew immediately which one must be mine.

A visitor with special intentions had clearly visited the office over the summer in the absence of its occupants to be. The office had been freshly painted in deep orange with touches of bright yellow trim. A poster was mounted above the desk directly across from the doorway. The poster caught the colors of the office walls. Or maybe, the colors of the office walls picked up the orange, yellow and pink glows of a sunset sky overhanging an empty beach, empty that is, except for a silhouetted couple walking hand in hand along the shoreline.

Interesting, I mused to myself, suspecting that an enamored girlfriend of Alejandro might be the interior decorator responsible for this un-academic like remake of graduate student study quarters. Amused, I proceeded to arrange my books and papers on the desk with no poster inspiring it. Once installed, I took a seat and began to read. The conditions for working seemed to be ideal: cool, quiet, and without distractions. I felt focused and alert.

After about thirty minutes of reading, I noticed that something was not quite right because the printed words on the page in front of me seemed to be jumping out at me like characters in a 3-D movie.

What's going on? Am I noticing the flickering fluorescent light accentuated by the low hissing the bulb makes? When I lifted my eyes from the dancing words on the open book, I noticed that the orange walls felt like a heavy blanket wrapping itself around me. This was definitely the sensation of claustrophobia.

With all the persistence I could muster I continued to read. However, the words just wouldn't stay in their proper place and the pages of the book were beginning to glow faintly orange. How am I ever going to work in this "romantic" space, I asked myself? Impatiently, I collected my books and papers, marching out of the office, upstairs and into the bright glare of the afternoon sun. Ah, this felt so much better. So where should I go next? Home to my bedroom in Escondido Village, where the portable Smith-Corona typewriter is waiting to be used. And that's where I would write the dissertation over the next six months word by word.

# SANTA CLAUS MEETS SOJOURNER TRUTH

Friday morning before Christmas, 1973, while tapping away on the Smith-Corona, putting the finishing touches on a chapter of the dissertation, the telephone rang. I stopped typing, ran downstairs and answered the call. Nancy, Chalyn's teacher at Sojourner Truth Children's Center, begins speaking in a panicked voice.

"Hi, Sherry, I am calling because Santa Claus has cancelled, and we don't know what we're going to do about the Christmas party this afternoon. Do you think that Robert might be able to be Santa?"

Just then, Robert walked in the door.

"Hey, Robert, come here, Nancy's on the phone and wants to ask you something," I call out to him.

Robert immediately agreed to be Santa Claus. Right away he left to pick up the Santa Claus suit at the costume shop. Helping him dress up in the big red suit, to make him look fat like Santa, I stuffed two

183

pillows into the suit then pulled the wide, shiny black, patent leather belt tightly over the pillows so they wouldn't slide down to his knees. The funniest part of the costume was the long, curly, white beard and moustache that he placed over his own dark moustache and beard. Of course, there was a red Santa's cap with a fat white tassel on it and a pair of big, black boots for his feet.

While driving to Sojourner Truth in our red Chevy II sleigh, he practiced his Santa Claus' laugh, "Ho, ho, ho." The center, named after Sojourner Truth, the noted African-American escaped slave who helped many other slaves flee from the South, was established by several progressive educators who were committed to high quality, low cost childcare for working families in the Palo Alto area. Sojourner Truth was an ideal place for Chalyn to spend most of the day while Robert and I wrote. The teachers were creative, loving and practiced a play-based curriculum for young children.

Arriving at Sojourner Truth, I went in first, so no one would suspect that I was coming with Santa Claus. The children, teachers and parents waited excitedly for Santa's arrival. When Robert came bouncing in, laughing his best Santa Claus laugh, I watched carefully to see if Chalyn recognized her daddy dressed up as Mr. Claus. But she didn't say anything.

Santa sat down on a chair in the middle of the room. Teacher Nancy, explained to the children that they would take turns telling Santa what they wanted for Christmas. She encouraged them to go up one by one to Santa, sit on his lap and talk to him. Most of the children hung back shyly. Then Nancy took

Kwame's hand leading him up to Santa. Santa Robert reached over to lift Kwame onto his lap, but Kwame resisted. He didn't want to sit on Santa's lap. He did, however, manage to tell Santa that he wanted a Tonka Bulldozer for Christmas. Then Santa gave Kwame a red and white striped candy cane.

After that a few of the other children approached Santa telling him what they wanted for Christmas. When it was Chalyn's turn, something different happened. Chalyn walked right up to Santa and practically jumped into his lap! She snuggled in Santa's lap telling him that she wanted a baby doll for Christmas. And, moreover, if she gets a baby doll she will call her "Elizabeth." Santa Robert laughed his best Santa's "Ho, Ho, Ho!" promising to try to bring her a baby doll for Christmas. Then he gave a striped candy cane to Chalyn. She grabbed it, but didn't want to stop sitting in Santa's lap. Teacher Nancy told her that it was time to let another child talk to Santa. Reluctantly, Chalyn climbed down. I kept expecting her to say, "You're not Santa, you're Daddy." But she never did. When we reached home that evening, she kept talking about how she sat in Santa's lap and told Santa that she wants a baby doll for Christmas.

# THE FINISH LINE

The dissertation clock continues ticking. Each morning I wake up thinking, "more to write today". Treating the work of writing as if it were a 9 to 5 job, I just keep at it, day in and day out. Gradually, the pages turn into chapters and the chapters shape into a book. Life seems to be a juggling act oscillating from writing to Chalyn and Robert, friends, political activities, and study groups and the bare minimum of domesticity to keep life afloat. There are never seemed to be enough hours in one day.

Being the kind of person who doesn't want to overlook brushing my teeth twice each day, getting at least seven hours of sleep each night, and regular exercise of any kind: running, swimming, volleyball, tennis or squash, there isn't any down time. However, I like it that way; it suits my do, do, do temperament.

Even as daily life proceeds, I am thinking about the next step in my life. I don't feel pulled back to Jamaica. I love my life at Stanford so much that I don't really want to leave. Of course, this is completely unrealistic. Departure is inevitable once the dissertation is finished and the fellowship comes to an end.

While I have been encouraged to apply for jobs in the States by my advisors, Robert, however, is in a big hurry to get back to his work with the Jamaican government. This is what people refer to many years later as "the two body" problem. How to find two satisfying, professional jobs in the same place at the same time?

Above all, I feel obligated to return to the Caribbean as part of a bargain I made with myself before coming to Stanford. After all, I reasoned, Robert came to Stanford with me, shouldn't I go back to Jamaica with him? Despite the realization that I am very grateful for what I learned in Jamaica, I can't quite visualize making a life there into an indefinite future.

Moreover, I do not want to return to a job with the Jamaican Government. Rejecting the possibility of another government job, I am left with only one other possibility, the university. When I tell Elizabeth Cohen, one of my dissertation advisers that I would be returning to an academic position at the University of the West Indies's faculty of education, she commented incredulously, "You're going to that back water?"

Her response gave me pause, and I reflected on what seemed like parochialism. At twenty-eight, I was still learning that life brings many compromises along with its surprises.  Returning to the West Indies would be among many of the compromises to be made over the coming years while trying to juggle two careers, a family, a marriage, friends and what tastes like an unquenchable thirst to know the world.

By early May my dissertation was written and accepted.  Getting ready to embark on the next phase of life as a professional woman raised a question that I had taken for granted until getting involved in the women's movement in the early 1970s.  The question posed was,

"What will be my name?"

Second wave feminism was influential in terms of raising this question: Where do our names come from, especially our "last" names? Feminists answered this question by saying that women's last names are part of the legacy of patriarchy. Derived from our fathers and their fathers and our father's grandfathers, I followed the dictates of tradition when getting married by changing my last name to my husband's. At the time, this seemed like a positive switch. My maiden name was neither easy to pronounce nor elegant.  It meant "wood hand" in German and was derived from my paternal great-great grandfather, a mid 19th century immigrant from Germany.  Girling, an English name, came from Robert's paternal great grandparents who migrated from Ipswich, England to Jamaica in the late 19th century.  While "Girling" is not common, at least it is pronounceable.

At this moment I am not feeling the least bit dissatisfied with Girling as my last name.  At the same time, I long for my own name identity. The names given to me at birth were Sherry Keith

Holtzclaw. My parents never explained why they chose "Sherry"; however, I always liked this name. "Keith", my middle name, came from my grandparents, Scottish in origin, and was also my father's middle name. In elementary school, classmates teased me because I had a "boy's" name for my middle name. At that time, I felt embarrassed because it was different than Sherry Sue or Sherry Jane, the typical middle names of most girls I knew. Now, at the moment I was about to be awarded my doctorate and embark on a career, Keith seemed like a plausible last name. Keith, unlike Holtzclaw, was an easy name to spell and pronounce. Hence, my decision was to become Sherry Keith.

My father-in-law was in a state of consternation over this "feminist" act. Nonetheless, he managed to take it with his characteristic good humor, needling a bit and referring to me as "Shelley Keats". I liked the joke which revealed him to be a true product of the British colonial education he underwent in late 1920s Jamaica.

# REGGAE & REVOLUTION (1974 - 1975)

*Dear Ariel and Zahava,*

*In July of 1974 we leave Stanford and California. We have one-way tickets to Kingston. My feelings are mixed: I am glad to be finished with studies, but sad to be letting go of four rich years brimming with new ideas, friends and experiences. We sell the red Chevy II to Aunt Leslie. Grandpa Billie doesn't want us leaving momentos in his garage. Under pressure, I discard my treasured blue eyed, auburn haired Ginny doll along with her red suitcase wardrobe. On the one hand, I think that Grandpa Billie is sad that we are leaving and the other, I think that he'd kind of like to go back to Jamaica with us.*

*Granny Sherry*

Chalyn & Bumbles, patio at Irish Town, 1974

# REGGAE AND REVOLUTION

Jamaica, in 1974, throbs with the sounds of reggae and the rhetoric of revolution. Jimmy Cliff's album, "The Harder They Come", followed by the film portraying a young black Jamaican's dream to become rich and famous finds a counterpoint in Bob Marley's music of Rastafarianism and Africanicity. The government of Michael Manley, a declared democratic socialist holds the reigns of political power.

Manley leads the Peoples National Party (PNP. Both parties, the PNP and the JLP (Jamaica Labour Party), have their roots in the trade union movement that emerged in the late 1930s. Manley's father, Norman is referred to as "the father of the nation". The middle class and intellectuals along with certain elements of the trade union movement support the PNP. The JLP is supported primarily by the working class and the unemployed poor in the slums of Kingston.

The country is increasingly divided between those who support an independent foreign policy, more services for the poor and needy. Some economists insist that a much greater share of the profits from foreign enterprises like the bauxite companies and tourism should remain in the country. Others believe Jamaica should continue its strong ties with Britain, Canada, and the United States and follow the Puerto Rican Boot Strap model of development.

In 1974, the Manley government decides to pass a special tax on the bauxite companies to increase revenues. Inspired by OPEC (the Organization of Petroleum Countries) Jamaica becomes instrumental in organizing an international association of bauxite producers around the world. Coupled with Michael Manley's staunch support of the non-aligned nations movement Fidel Castro's Cuba, Jamaica's closest neighbor, the PNP government is rapidly losing popularity with middle class Jamaicans primarily oriented to North America or England. This begins to weigh heavily on the political relationship between Jamaica and the United States.

Robert returned to work with the GOJ. The Central Planning Unit, upgraded and expanded under the Manley government, is now the National Planning Agency. He becomes one of several deputy directors of planning, reporting directly to the Prime Minister. The job throws challenges from every point on the development compass. Put in charge of the "Special Employment Program" with unemployment at nearly 20 percent of the work force, job creation is headlined as a top economic and political priority. Meeting regularly with the upper tier of the Jamaican leadership, he finds himself in the thick of the social democratic policies central to Manley's agenda.

As soon as we return to Jamaica, we have a house on the university campus thanks to the help of our friend Marlene Manderson-Jones, now assistant registrar at the University of the West Indies. It's large, empty and allows me to ride my bicycle to my office on the campus situated in an airy, old colonial house—a former professor's home—not far from the Faculty of Education. Enclosed in a small porch with windows on three sides and French doors opening into the garden filled with big mango, lignum vitae, and acacia trees, I couldn't be happier with my working quarters which are always light filled and airy even on the hottest day.

I am part of an interdisciplinary faculty team charged with the responsibility of delivering an in-service course for secondary school teachers with no background in education. The teachers will come from all over the island, and the classes must take place during the teachers' vacation periods as well as bi-weekly meetings on Fridays. My part of the curriculum is to include segments on comparative education and educational research. This is my first teaching job, and I feel quite nervous. I am teaching teachers, most of who are older than I with considerably more classroom experience. However, imbued with youthful energy, good intentions, and provocative ideas, I arrive ready to dive into the work. My colleagues prove to be friendly and supportive, so all in all this is a good place to begin a career.

Still, I miss my friends and life at Stanford tremendously. And because of the unusual teaching schedule, I have quite a bit of free time on my hands. I begin to attend lectures held on the university campus organized by Trevor Munroe and others who are trying to build a political party to the left of the Peoples National Party. They are studying basic Marxism in a quite fundamentalist fashion. While curious to learn what they are about, after a bit of exposure, I don't feel at all drawn to this group. They are just too orthodox for my political tastes.

Verandah conversations with Robert's relatives focus mostly on the fear of violence and dissatisfaction with the Manley government. More and more middle class people are barricading themselves into their homes with iron bar grills on the windows, the doors, the verandas and even putting wrought iron doors between the living area of their houses and the bedrooms which they lock before going to sleep at night. While many people owned "one bad dog when we first came to live in Jamaica six years ago, now it is common to own a whole pack of "bad dogs" that will rush any visitors who step foot on their property.

The fear of violence spreads like an uncontrolled infection. I have never experienced any problems living in Jamaica. Why should worry plague me now? Frequently, Robert travels throughout the island staying away overnight. The spacious house on the Mona campus is completely grill-free with large glass doors that open onto the verandah and unkempt garden beyond. Anyone walking along the Mona Road can see into the curtain-less windows. At night with the lights on, I feel like I am living in a fish bowl.

Yearning for the quite, cool and far from the maddening crowd atmosphere of Irish Town, I propose that we move out of Kingston back to the Blue Mountains where a sense of peace and calm prevail. Instead of moving to Mandala Cottage, we find an elegant, two-story house with sweeping views. French doors in the living room open onto a patio and garden. Mauvis Bank and Guava Ridge stare at us across the deep valley. On a clear day, Blue Mountain Peak reveals itself to the east. To the west the mountains drop away and the Mona Reservoir lies quietly behind a low ridge of hills separating it from the coast. "Beverly Hills" covers the far tip of the ridge. On the horizon beyond Mona, Beverly Hills and the Kingston plain, at the tip of the Palisades, fading into the Caribbean Sea is Port Royal, home of infamous 17th and 18th century pirates like Long John Silver. The sea stretches across the horizon, turquoise blue in the morning; silver, gold in the afternoon and shimmering black at night.

Reaching Irish Town involves a journey. One hundred fifty eight turns switch back and forth along the mountainside on the narrow road from Papine Market to our house just across the road from Bamboo Lodge. Despite the arduousness of the journey I want to live there . The mountains, cool and calm, soothe me. Irish Town feels so much safer than Kingston without need for grills on the windows and doors. Once installed, we can sit comfortably on the porch enjoying the beautiful views anytime, day or night.

~

Of course, with both Robert and I working in town the logistics of life multiply. Annabel Foster-

Davis, Robert's cousin, who lives down the hill a bit, helps us find a housekeeper/babysitter. Our housekeeper's name is Mazie. She is what Jamaicans refer to as "red". Her skin and hair gleam bright amber against her dark, comforting, brown eyes. She's nineteen, tall, strong, but already missing several front teeth from too much sugar and no dental care

From the beginning, I invite Mazie to sit down and eat meals with us. She doesn't object. We talk about her family. Both parents are farmers who grow banana and vegetables on the steep hillsides of the Blue Mountains. Mazie is one of seven children, sandwiched somewhere in the middle. Mazie finished primary school, but hasn't gone on to high school. Clearly, it's difficult for Jamaican teenagers who live in "the country". The only schools Mazie could attend are down in Kingston and the bus fare to town would cost more than her family could afford.

Several days each week, I work at home. The room used as a study has an eight by eight foot plate glass window with a 180-degree view of the Blue Mountains and Kingston/St. Andrew plain below. This is where I prepare classes and write. Together, Robert and I have made a long desktop out of a door. It's a spectacular place to work. There's a sandy white overstuff chair for comfortable reading. It turns out to be an amusingly organic chair. Shortly after we move in I notice there's a plant sprouting from the creases between the cushion and the armrest. Upon closer inspection, I notice that the plant looks suspiciously like "ganja", the Jamaican term for marijuana. Robert has also discovered similar plants around the yard where he's been growing tomatoes.

One morning, sitting in the study while preparing my classes, I heard a small child's voice calling, "Anne, Anne, Anne, come na Anne."

Looking out the picture window, I saw Mazie appear at the garden wall looking over the edge of the terrace. Just minutes later, she came into the study asking if she could go home for a while, reporting that her mother needed some help.

About an hour later, Mazie returned. Curious about the small voice calling out, "Anne, Anne..." I asked her,

"Who was that calling you, Maize?"

"Oh, that's me brader, ma'm."

"Why was he calling you Anne?"

"That's me name, ma'm."

I am totally confused.

"Then why did you tell us to call you Mazie if it's not your name?"

"Because de las place me work, de mistress did call me, Mazie."

"Why did she call you Mazie?" This was something I really wanted to know.

"Well, when I go fe work and tell she me name is Anne, she say she don't like that name and will call me Mazie."

"Well, what do you like to be called?" was my next question.

"I like Anne."

"Then we'll call you Anne."

# A TROPICAL STORM

This story happens on a Tuesday. Each Tuesday morning, Robert and I drive Chalyn and her friend Matthew to Mt. Mercy Academy where they go to pre-school. We take turns chauffeuring the children with our neighbors, Heidi and John. On the days that I teach, Robert and I drive Chalyn and Matthew to school, and John, Matt's dad, picks them up in the early afternoon. That way Robert and I can stay the entire day in Kingston working then return to Irish Town in the evening. On the afternoons when we aren't home, Chalyn stays with Anne and often plays with Matt and his little brother, James.

Mt. Mercy is a Catholic school run by Maltese nuns. Just like the nuns in the movie "Heidi", the nuns wear black and white costumes with big hats that hide their hair. The children also wear uniforms: Chalyn wears a blue and white checked jumper, a white blouse with puffy sleeves and white socks in blue tennis shoes. Matthew uses the same blue and white checked shirt with a pair blue shorts.

At the entrance to Mt Mercy Academy life size statutes of Snow White and the Seven Dwarfs await the children's arrival. Maybe the statues have been placed there to placate the children. Or maybe to reassure their parents that the school is a child friendly place. I never become entirely convinced that this is the kind of school I desire for my daughter. (Many years later, Chalyn told me that the teacher sometimes hit her hand with a ruler if she didn't know the right answer to a question. What regret I felt upon hearing this. If I'd known, I would have taken her out of the Mt. Mercy Academy immediately.)

On one particular Tuesday afternoon, I am attending a meeting of the In-Service Diploma in Education faculty. Seven of us are gathered together in the director's office strategizing about how to organize the students' research projects. While we talk, the sky begins to blacken very quickly. Around 3 o'clock, the wind starts charging through the trees that surround the building. Soon the trees start to creak and howl in response to the wind. All of us try to stay focused on the work at hand. However, it's more and more difficult to ignore the angry wind racing around outside. Suddenly, we hear a loud crack, which sounds like a gigantic firecracker. A deep thud follows the crack.

Looking at each other with startled faces, the conversation stops. Maybe a tree branch snapped and fell onto the roof? With each moment the sky grows thicker with menace. The air feels oppressively heavy. Then rain bursts from the closed sky. There isn't anything shy or subtle about this rain. Giant raindrops pelt the roof and the windows, like pounding nails. The growing fury around us can no longer be ignored. Pauline goes to call her husband. She comes back reporting that the streets all over Kingston are starting to flood.

Then Cecil Gray, our silver haired director, calmly suggests we adjourn the meeting so people can go home.

I want to leave, but can't. I have to wait for Robert to come pick me up, so we can drive to Irish Town. The rain keeps beating on the roof and assaulting the windows. The wind continues to howl through the trees. I wait. It's four o'clock. Then it's four thirty. Now it's five o'clock, then five fifteen. Finally it's five thirty. Through the continuing down pour, I spot a small, white Ford Escort pulling into the driveway. Grabbing my things, I dash through the downpour, jumping into the car.

"Everything's flooded between here and Kingston. It's a tropical storm." Robert's wide eyes look a bit frightened. "It took me over an hour to get from the Planning Agency to the university. Cars are stopped all over in flooded intersections. We won't be able to drive up to Irish Town now. It's too dangerous. We just have to try to make it to Ruby and Stanton's place and wait there until the rain stops."

"What about Chalyn?" I exclaim, feeling nearly panicked.

"Well, hopefully, Anne will take care of her. Since there's no telephone, there's nothing we can do."

SHERRY KEITH

I realized that he's right. We didn't have a telephone in Irish Town, and we certainly couldn't drive all the way up the mountain in a tropical storm.

Once at Donhead Avenue, Granny Ruby tries to reassure us and then recalls the old Jamaican rhyme, "June too soon, July stand by, August get ready, September hold steady, October it's all over." All through the night I listen to the rain beat on the zinc roof like a snare drummer's war march. At first I doubt that I will ever sleep. I am thinking about Chalyn, wondering if she's with Anne, and what's happening in Irish Town. Eventually, I fall asleep to the incessant drumming of the rain.

The next morning, the sun was grinning in through the bedroom window while the parakeets chirped in the garden. Mr. Ed, the donkey, brayed as usual, insisting on an old carrot and wilted lettuce – his daily morning treats. The tropical storm had evaporated like a bad dream that disappears with daylight. Both Robert and I are so anxious to get up to Irish Town that we don't bother to eat breakfast. Now the roads in Kingston look dry as an old bone. Where has the tropical storm gone?

As we drive, snaking up the Irish Town road, the mountains testify that the tropical storm has really been here. Bamboo plumes lay broken on the hillsides. Mud streams cross the road where large rocks and tree branches lay scattered. Rounding a sharp curve, maybe a half mile below our house, huge boulders and a downed No. 11 mango tree block the road.

We stop, get out of the Escort and start to walk as fast as we can uphill. When we reach our house, Anne is there waiting. Chalyn, however, isn't with her.

"She go with Miss Heidi to Bamboo Lodge yesterday after school. Dem stay dere."

We charge over to Bamboo Lodge asking for Heidi and the children. We're directed to the apartment where they have all gone to stay. Heidi, James and Matt greet us at the door. But where is Chalyn? We are worried again. In the apartment we discover Chalyn hiding in a closet. She's having so much fun playing with Matt and James that she doesn't want to come home with us!

Heidi explained that the rains were so heavy that she and John feared their little hillside cottage might slide. At this point they decided to flee to Bamboo Lodge taking Chalyn with them—knowing that we wouldn't be able to get home that night.

All's well that ends well, so Shakespeare says. Chalyn has had a sleep over with Matt and James. Heidi and John decide to move to Bamboo Lodge permanently. We are very happy to have them so close that the children can play any time they wish. And today is a Wednesday in October, which means, as far as hurricanes and tropical storms go, it's all over.

# POSTSCRIPT

*Dear Ariel and Zahava,*

*In January, an invitation from Isaura and Glaura, our Stanford classmates and veterans of the Escondido Village dinner co-op, arrives in Jamaica. Isaura and Glaura are inviting Robert and me to come to the Federal University of Minas Gerais in Belo Horizonte, Brazil as visiting professors. They want our help developing the new graduate program in education and the social sciences, which they founded upon their return from Stanford.*

*What an exciting opportunity is my reaction! Robert is less enthusiastic. At this moment, he's content with his work as Deputy Director of National Planning. However I feel like an outsider in this newborn post-colonial society which seems to be exploding with political, social, racial and cultural tensions. These are the same tensions that the song writer/performer Bob Marley tells the world about in songs like, "I Shot the Sheriff, but I Didn't Shoot the Deputy"; "Get Up Stand Up Stand Up for Your Rights" and "No Woman, No Cry".*

*Brazil offers the possibility of a new beginning and the opportunity to make a difference working with friends we know and trust. I am intent on giving Brazil a try. After the academic year finishes I leave Jamaica for Stanford. Rina Benmajor, then assistant professor of Spanish at Stanford and a good friend, arranges for me to audit a summer intensive course in Portuguese. Joaquim Coelho, also a professor at Stanford and a native of Brazil, is the teacher. He uses the tried and true audio-lingual method of teaching language. The course includes four hours daily of classes, plus the language lab exercises for eight weeks.*

*"Da janela vejo um pedaco da praia," (From the window I see a bit of the beach—presumably Ipanema in Rio de Janeiro) is the first phrase I learn to say in Portuguese. Followed by, "Pao fresco engorda!" (Fresh bread makes you fat!—please don't ever forget that, it's absolutely true.)*

*By the end of these eight weeks, we students can barely speak Portuguese, but are well on our way to learning. And then it's time to get ready to go to Brazil. That, however, is another story that I will tell you about some other time.*

*Granny Sherry*

# ABOUT THE AUTHOR

Sherry Keith was born and grew up in California. At the age of nineteen she took her first extended travel: a three month summer trip around Europe. Prior to living in Jamaica, she studied sociology at the University of California, Berkeley then moved to England for graduate studies in the sociology of literature at University of Essex. With her Jamaican-born husband, she moved to the Caribbean. Here she began a career in educational development working for the Government of Jamaica. During this period, she intermittently returned to California to complete a doctorate in International Development Education at Stanford University. After seven years in the Caribbean, she immigrated with her family to Brazil. Later she worked throughout the Americas as an education specialist for the World Bank and other international organizations. Still traveling but now settled in Berkeley, California, she has been a faculty member at San Francisco State University since 1989.